"So many people just exist without clear direction. It's my life's ... develop a vision and achieve their dreams and goals. That's why I'm so excited about this wonderful book from Jennifer Ford Berry. In *Make Room*, you get a step-by-step guide on how to live a fulfilled and happy life as you discover and pursue your God-given purpose."

Terri Savelle Foy, founder of Terri Savelle Foy Ministries and author of 5 *Things Successful People Do Before 8 A.M.*

"In a world that keeps us drowning in excess—yet still acquiring more—we need strategies for mindful and intentional living. In this compelling, well-timed guide, Jennifer Ford Berry shows us how to wisely steward the gifts God gives us and create space to breathe. Beyond making room in your home, it will make room in your heart, mind, and soul. Yes, it is possible to choose purpose over possessions—and this book shows you exactly how."

Kari Kampakis, author of *Love Her Well* and *More Than a Mom*

"This book is brilliantly written. I love how Jennifer uses her gift of organizing to teach us how to create as well as embrace alignment in our lives. This book details the steps needed to not only organize our rooms, closets, and drawers but also our lives in such a way that we experience freedom and flow more purposefully in every step we take."

Jacinda Jacobs, author of *Uniquely Qualified* and motivational speaker

"Jennifer does an incredible job of laying out practical steps for success in faith and life, showing the importance of how they weave together and the impact they have on our lives and the lives around us."

Amy Debrucque, author of *Embolden* and host of the *Life On Purpose* podcast

"I firmly believe every person, at some time in their life, has to ask themselves a vital question: Is this all there is? In *Making Room*, Jennifer Ford Berry not only answers this question but also gives a clear strategy to help readers get rid of the limitations in life and become all God has created them to be. Warning: do not read this book unless you want your life to explode to brand-new proportions!"

Hannah Keely, America's #1 mom coach, founder of Mom Mastery University, bestselling author, speaker, and host of the public broadcasting series *Hannah, Help Me!*

"While I've never been a fan of clutter, I've definitely been guilty of putting too much stock in gaining material things. I'm sure I'm not the only one. Thankfully, in *Make Room*, Jennifer graciously challenges us to value purpose over possessions. She dares us to dream about the right things and helps us to declutter not only our drawers but the darkest corners of our hearts, so that we can make room to fully invite God and others in. When we choose to discover and live out our purpose, rather than chasing possessions, we invest in what truly matters. Matthew 6:19 encourages us not to store up for ourselves treasures on earth, where moth and rust destroy. Jennifer understands the merit in this truth, and will inspire you to treasure and invest in the things that give the most rewarding returns."

Danielle Macaulay, author, speaker, creator of the *Married Up* podcast, and TV personality on the marriage enrichment show *A Better Us*

"*Make Room* is a blessing for readers in every season of life as we navigate through messaging and marketing that wants us to believe our lives and homes should look a certain way. Jennifer's guidance—from the bigger picture to the smaller how-to steps—helps us purge literal and spiritual clutter in such a clear way that readers will walk away feeling clarity before they've even touched a single possession."

Lori Beth Auldridge, MA, MFA, host
of the *Elevating Motherhood* podcast

"Jennifer writes with tremendous passion and purpose! Her ability to capture the heartbeat behind stewarding our lives well is what gives this book such power. You won't just walk away with a practical to-do list but with a strong 'why' to back it up and sustain it for the long haul. You'll feel like you have a personal organizer in your corner, rooting for you, guiding you, and ultimately pointing you to Christ, your ultimate reason to steward your life with excellence!"

Laura Dudek, founder of Ruah + Ember, author,
and Christian speaker

"Jennifer is a thoughtful, caring organizer and life-changer. Her approach to organizing will help you not only in your home but also in your treasured family relationships and the rest of your life. I highly recommend her if you are searching for peace and calm in your home sanctuary."

Jen Kilbourne Obermeier, founder
of Pro Organizer Studio

"This book is so much more than a decluttering handbook. It's an invitation to live with intention and to step into your God-given purpose and live it out through your home, possessions, priorities, and life in general. Through Scripture, heartfelt prayers, and practical insights, *Make Room* will inspire you to live a fuller, more joyful, and meaningful life."

Marielle Melling, author of *Peace amidst the Mayhem* and founder of Lovin' Life with Littles

MAKE
ROOM

MAKE ROOM

Take Control of Your
Space, Time, Energy, and Money
to Live on Purpose

Jennifer Ford Berry

BakerBooks
a division of Baker Publishing Group
Grand Rapids, Michigan

© 2022 by Jennifer Ford Berry

Published by Baker Books
a division of Baker Publishing Group
PO Box 6287, Grand Rapids, MI 49516-6287
www.bakerbooks.com

Printed in the United States of America

Library of Congress Cataloging-in-Publication Data
Names: Berry, Jennifer Ford, 1975– author.
Title: Make room : take control of your space, time, energy, and money to live on purpose / Jennifer Ford Berry.
Description: Grand Rapids, MI : Baker Books, a division of Baker Publishing Group, [2022]
Identifiers: LCCN 2021056245 | ISBN 9781540902153 (paperback) | ISBN 9781493437542 (ebook)
Subjects: LCSH: Simplicity—Religious aspects—Christianity.
Classification: LCC BV4647.S48 B47 2022 | DDC 241/.68—dc23/eng/20211130
LC record available at https://lccn.loc.gov/2021056245

The author is represented by the literary agency of Wordwise Media Services.

Baker Publishing Group publications use paper produced from sustainable forestry practices and post-consumer waste whenever possible.

22 23 24 25 26 27 28   7 6 5 4 3 2 1

Contents

Acknowledgments

First of all, to God: thank you for giving me a vision for this book and for giving me the courage to take my writing in this direction. Thank you for guiding me to live out my purpose each and every day. Please bless each person reading this book and help them find their way to the unique purpose you have already declared for them.

To my children, Randsley and Bryceton: God has anointed each of you with a specific set of skills, personality, and spirit for your assignment here on earth. He will send people, resources, gifts, and visions to help you achieve his dreams for you. Please do not waste it. I hope this book inspires you to run after it with your whole life and never stop.

To my husband, Josh: I would not be able to live out my purpose each and every day without your support, love, and sacrifice. I am so proud of our marriage and the life we have created. I am eternally grateful that God brought us together for this life.

Introduction

Do you feel overwhelmed because of everything you need to get done in a day? Are you exhausted from trying to take care of all the stuff you have accumulated in your life? Do you lack fulfillment? Do you feel stuck?

If so, you are not alone. I have met with hundreds of people just like you over the years, and I am here to tell you there is another way, a better way, to go through this life. If you are finding you have less and less time and energy to spend on the things you enjoy doing, chances are you need to make a change. God did not create you so that you could work to gain more possessions and then be a slave to them. He does not want you to feel overwhelmed and stressed out. He wants you to have abundance in joy, peace, and love, not just have more stuff.

Our society has been told over and over that more possessions or better possessions will make us happier, healthier, or more successful. It's simply not true, but we continue to keep trying to prove it will work. We spend the majority of our lives working so we can earn money. Then we use the

13

majority of that money to pay for the biggest home we can, which we continuously fill with stuff that is supposed to improve our lives in some way but always leaves us feeling empty.

I recently started working with a brand-new client. I pulled up to a gorgeous new house complete with a line of shiny cars in the driveway, lush landscaping, and a resort-like pool in the backyard. She met me in the driveway, where we spoke for about twenty minutes. During that conversation, she admitted how much she missed her previous home, so much so that she and her husband decided not to sell it but instead kept it and rented it out. I commented on how gorgeous her new home was and asked why she felt she was missing the previous one so much. She kept telling me about the memories there. That house was the one where she raised three children and created a life with her husband, and times had been simpler.

I wish I had a $100 bill for each time I've heard a story like this. Believe it or not, it is very common. I think it is because we are told if we have *more*, we will be happier. The truth, however, is different.

Not only does more and more stuff provide less and less joy as time goes on but it can also make us start to feel resentful. Why? Because everything we bring into our lives costs us something: space, time, energy, money, or all of the above! If you don't believe me, look around your home and take note of the different tasks required for each item you own. Look at how much space you are giving up and how much money you are spending just on maintenance. Then ask yourself if these things still make you happy. I guarantee some do, but most don't.

■ ■ ■ ■ ■

You have a purpose assigned to your life, a divine, God-given purpose that has nothing to do with what you own. This purpose is perfectly matched to your gifts, skills, and personality. God has had it in mind for your life since before you were even born. If you can figure out what your purpose is and start spending more time and effort on that—and less on your stuff—you will be a much happier person. I can only imagine how different this world would be if more of us were committed to living out our unique purpose in alignment with God's will.

If you picked up this book, I have to guess you are wondering what it looks like to choose your purpose over your possessions in the world we live in today. Well, I can tell you that it is a lifestyle choice, one that is filled with intention and free of clutter.

As a professional organizer for almost two decades, I have been in hundreds of homes. I have arrived at beautiful, immaculate houses full of every possession you can imagine only to meet another person at the door who begins by explaining how overwhelmed they are. They are usually exhausted from trying to maintain all of their belongings, and they think that if I can just organize it all for them, life will be so much better. To a certain extent, this is true. An organized home *will* make you happier, give you an energy boost, and save you lots of time. And trust me, I love providing that service. (In fact, I have written a three-book series called Organize Now! that provides step-by-step plans to get every area of your life and your home organized.)

But each time we begin the process of getting our things organized, there is a more profound process going on inside our spirits. The process of letting go of that which does not serve us is a very empowering and liberating experience. Getting organized forces us to face each of the items we have brought into our homes. It makes us realize how much stuff we actually have—and how much of that stuff we do not need or use. Somewhere in the process, we begin to realize that what we truly want is more freedom, more contentment, more time for things we love to do, and more space to breathe.

I love helping people get their closets and cabinets organized. But what I love even more is teaching people how to live with intention and purpose. Intention can help us define what is important. Purpose gives us a reason to stick with the process. When we have both of these, it is easier to remove everything that does not belong.

■ ■ ■ ■ ■

I have a gift for seeing potential in people and spaces. I have used the principles taught in this book to help transform hundreds of lives, including my own, and I have lived out my own journey of choosing purpose over possessions over the past twenty years. As an organized person, I love a good plan and, to be blatantly honest, I like to be in control. My original plan for my life included moving from western New York to southern Florida for college, so that I could obtain a degree in business and marketing that would enable me to work in corporate America and make a lot of money.

Shortly after graduation, I moved to Charlotte, North Carolina, because of its booming job market. There, I made it to corporate America and had the paycheck I always wanted, but I still didn't feel fulfilled. Then my plans shifted drastically. I was standing in the newsroom at Clear Channel Radio where I worked on that unforgettable day: September 11, 2001. As we all watched those planes crash into the World Trade Center, I was horrified, and I remember thinking I did not want to waste another minute in my life. A few months later, I was laid off from that job due to cutbacks and became an unemployed new mom. I knew I wanted to do more with my life. Sure, I still wanted to make money and have nice things, but I also wanted to wake up every morning and do something that mattered.

While strolling through a bookstore one day, I picked up a book called *Do What You Love, the Money Will Follow: Discovering Your Right Livelihood* by Marsha Sinetar. I'll be honest, at first I laughed, thinking, *Yeah, right. How am I going to do what I love and still make money?* Throughout the book, Marsha kept asking, "What are you passionate about?"[1] I had to answer many questions about myself. Each time I was honest with myself about my passion, the words *organizing* and *helping women* kept coming to the forefront of my mind. That was something that got me excited! My earliest memories include organizing. I organized my grandma's jewelry every time I visited her. I organized my bedroom continuously. I loved every aspect of organizing: improving space, sorting, implementing categories, and, most of all, the peace and joy I felt after I completed the work. This passion was something placed inside of me long before I was born. I just hadn't realized it yet.

Maybe you currently have a longing to do something more meaningful in your life but have no idea what that could be.

You are too distracted by all of the "clutter" in your life: tasks and responsibilities, stuff in your home and workspace, negative thoughts taking up space in your mind, or toxic relationships that are sucking the life right out of you.

Do you ever feel like you were supposed to be on a different path in life right now, but somehow life just keeps happening every day, without any intentional steps from you? If so, this book will help you begin to live a more intentional and purposeful life by teaching you how to strip away what is less important (aka *clutter*) in order to make room for what is more important.

Even when I started working as an organizer, I did not realize it would turn into a purpose. But after years of helping people get organized, I realized that my purpose was not to create "Pinterest-perfect" homes but to help others see what is most important and then help them build their home and their life around that. After all, God has made it so that we all enter and leave this earth empty-handed. We can continue to focus on accumulating things—but in the end, will that matter?

I share my story with you because I want you to find yourself in it somewhere. When God breathed life into you, he also breathed an idea into you, one that nobody else on the entire planet can do quite like you! Maybe you don't realize what that is right now, but there have been clues along the way. I want to help you find them and find out what your purpose is so you can start living it out every single day.

I am also passionate about teaching people to let go of the things they no longer love or use and give them to the people who need those exact items! Did you know there is probably a women's shelter in your community that could use those blankets in your hall closet that are collecting dust? And there are children nearby who would love the toys that have been sitting in your attic. I am not going to say you should give everything away and become a minimalist. I am going to encourage you to take a closer look at what you own and also encourage you to share the things you no longer love or need.

■ ■ ■ ■ ■

This book is divided into ten primary principles: possibilities, purpose, possessions, prepare, plan your time, part with clutter, practice stewardship, privileged giving, provide hospitality, and partner with God. When you apply these to your life, you will begin to see huge results. This book will teach you how to recognize and eliminate the clutter that may be distracting you from your God-given purpose. Each chapter will give you a strategy to live with more intention. It will teach you how to let go of things that are cluttering up your home and your mind, without feeling guilty.

If you picked up this book because you want to get excited about life again, I am super excited for you, because I know you are going to be transformed. There is an amazing plan waiting for you! I can't tell you that this book is going to have all the answers to your life-provoking questions or tell you exactly what to do with all of your things. But I can tell you it will inspire you to dream bigger, guide you to recognize clutter in your life, and teach you how to eliminate clutter piece by piece. You will learn how to gain more space, time, energy, and money in your life. Your mind will be opened up to new possibilities.

So go ahead: turn the page and dive in. By the end of this book, I hope you'll have figured out what your purpose is and find the courage you need to live it unapologetically for the rest of your life. Remember, we do not leave a legacy by buying things. We leave a legacy by doing things!

WHY WE MAKE ROOM

ONE

Possibilities

Jesus looked at them intently and said, "Humanly speaking,
it is impossible. But with God everything is possible."

Matthew 19:26

D o you believe that anything is possible in life? I mean,
truly believe it? Can you stop for a minute and wrap
your head around Jesus's words? "But with God everything is possible." He did not say some things. He said *everything*. This statement is not just for a celebrity, a preacher, or
your neighbor. This promise is for *all* of us. Each one of us,
even when we don't fully grasp it. Even when we don't understand it. Even when we don't believe it.

Friends, I know we can all have moments of unbelief in our
lives. But our disbelief never changes the promises of God.
And may I also remind you that God cannot lie! So, basically,
it is up to us to get on board with these promises, this way of
thinking, these possibilities for our lives. Otherwise, when
we miss the boat, we'll have no one to blame but ourselves.

Are you like I once was, laughing at the thought of making money doing what you love? I know there are times when the possibility of a situation getting better is hard to believe. I get it! I don't know your story, but I am sure it has led you to the opinions you currently have about this life.

If you do believe anything is possible, then I am giving you a huge high five right now, because that means you don't let heartache and disappointment steal your hope. Lord only knows the heartaches and frustrations you have endured. None of us can get through life without experiencing difficulties, and unfortunately, some of us seem to have to endure far greater suffering than others. But no matter what, we can still choose to believe in possibilities, especially if we believe in God. With him, all things are possible.

So right now, I want you to put all of your hesitation aside for just a bit and imagine new possibilities. Close your eyes for about five minutes, right now, and then pray this simple prayer while taking some deep breaths:

Lord, I ask that you give me a vision of all the possibilities for my life. Open my eyes in areas where I may be blind. Give me your wisdom and guidance. Help me to understand the life you intended for me when you created me. Show me my life from your perspective, Lord. In Jesus's name I pray, amen.

What's Your Vision?

A vision is a mental image of what the future could look like. When God created the universe, he imagined the possibilities in his mind. As Scripture tells us, "By faith we understand that the entire universe was formed at God's command, that what we now see did not come from anything that can be seen" (Heb. 11:3).

God created a specific vision, and then that vision became a reality. Isn't it amazing to think that the manifestation of God's imagination created everything we can now see with our physical eyes? And each of us, created in his image, also has an imagination to use.

In Kris Vallotton's book *Poverty, Riches and Wealth*, he writes: "There is something very powerful about your imagination. It is vision that shapes our lives and directs our destinies. What you imagine has a huge effect on who you are becoming. You are forming your outer world with your inner thoughts."[1]

For you to come up with a vision for your life, you must first imagine your own possibilities. A synonym of the word *possibility* is *hope*.[2] Think of something you have always hoped for that hasn't happened yet. Now imagine the possibility of it happening.

What would your life look like?

What would it change?

Who could you help?

What could it mean for the next generation of your family?

Now take it a step further and envision how you would feel about yourself if these things happened. Would you feel

proud?

content?

excited?
joyful?
relieved?

OK, you are ready. Take a few minutes to write down your hopes and dreams. Start to pray over this list daily. Put your faith in God that it will come to pass in his perfect timing.

Without imagining all of the possibilities, you will never be able to create a vision for your life. I like to think of a vision as a painted picture in your mind. One that will depict what you want your life to be. The more detail in the picture, the better!

Your vision is your *big why*. It's a compelling reason why you want to do something. It gives you direction, and it is your desired future. Your vision includes what you believe in (your core values). Having a vision will not only teach you how to be intentional with your life but can also change the course of your life forever.

Dream, Don't Doubt

When was the last time you let yourself sit and daydream? Hopefully recently! But I have found that many people haven't spent much time daydreaming since they were children.

When I was a little girl, I loved to climb trees. Since our home was surrounded by woods, I had an abundance of trees to choose from. I would sit up in those branches, away from everything, and dream. Not only was it incredibly peaceful but I could envision my dreams coming true as clearly as if I were watching a movie. It was so easy to do back then because I was less distracted than I am now. Plus, I gave myself time and permission to do it. I wasn't sitting in that tree thinking, *I'd better hurry up so I can get back to cleaning the house.*

It's true. As adults, we have less time and more responsibilities. But that doesn't mean we can't make time to daydream. As long as you are still breathing, you have work to do on this planet, and daydreaming will fill your mind with the possibilities. Jennie Allen says, "To get our hearts primed and ready to begin dreaming, we need to till the soil a little bit. Loosen up the hard parts and make room for the seeds to grow."[3]

I highly encourage you to set aside some time to think about all the possibilities for your life. Just let your imagination run wild! Ask yourself questions like these:

If you could do anything with your life, what would it be?

What are you most passionate about?

What do you love doing?

When are you the most joyful?

What have you always dreamed about doing?

What are your gifts?

What would you do if you knew you couldn't fail?

What could you contribute to the world that would make you feel proud or excited?

What kind of parent do you want to be?

What do you want your home to feel like?

What do you want more of?

What do you want less of?

How do you want to be remembered when you have left this earth?

Mark 9 tells a story about Jesus healing a demon-possessed boy. The father brings the boy to Jesus and begs for mercy. He asks if Jesus can help them. Jesus responds, "What do you mean 'If I can'?. . . Anything is possible if a person believes" (v. 23). The father instantly cries out, "I do believe, but help me overcome my unbelief!" (v. 24).

I have to admit, I feel so relieved when I read that passage because I, too, believe and yet still struggle with unbelief at times. Then I feel guilty for my disbelief. But guilt does not help me keep going when times are tough.

When we start to struggle with these feelings of doubt, that is the exact time we need to stop and cry out to God, "Lord, help me overcome my unbelief!" There are going to be days when you are very fired up about the possibilities for your life. But there will also be days on this journey toward a purpose that you will have doubts, and that is OK. When it happens, know that God is waiting and is willing to pour more faith onto you. Faith is a gift from God, and the more we rely on him, the more it grows.

Are you afraid of leaping into new possibilities? Are you afraid of what people will think? Does it feel like it is taking forever for your dream to come true?

I get you. I felt like I was lost in limbo for about two years. I was not writing. I lost my vision. I couldn't even think clearly. I completely lost my creativity. One day while I was in a Hobby Lobby, I picked up a framed quote (I love quotes) that said, "Things are about to get really good." I felt compelled to buy it, and I took it home and put it on my bathroom windowsill where I could see it every day. I didn't know what was going to happen, but I knew God had shown me that sign to remind me to keep my hope and faith in him. I read that sign so many times. Some days when I felt discouraged or impatient, I would think, *I guess this sign wasn't God, because nothing is happening.* Other days, my faith would be stronger and I would read it with every ounce of hope I had.

From Dream to Reality

Ready to dream? Here are a few tips to get you started.

1. Look beyond your current circumstances.

There are many seasons in life. For example, you may currently have small children who need you to be home with them so you can avoid daycare expenses. Looking beyond your current circumstances doesn't mean you have to leave them now, but soon you will move on to another season, such as when they go to school. I wrote my first published book when my younger child was napping and my older child was at preschool. Seasons keep changing, and life rolls along. You never know what the future might have in store for you.

2. Do not let other people's opinions direct your steps.

How many stories have you heard about successful people receiving a hundred "nos" before they got one "yes"? It happens all the time. God gives us all different opinions, personalities, and dreams for a reason. And guess what: this makes it difficult for us all to be on the same page at the same time. So it is 100 percent OK if nobody else in the world completely understands your dream. In fact, what other people think of your dream has nothing to do with whether or not you should pursue it. The truth is, if God put a dream in your heart, it is tied to the purpose he has planned for you. That's all you need to know.

3. Stop worrying about your own limitations.

If you have a dream in your heart, and there is no way you can accomplish it entirely on your own, chances are it is from God. He wants you to rely on him, and he wants you to ask for his help. These God-size dreams and possibilities are placed in our hearts so that we can be used to fulfill his goals, not our own. God has all the details already figured out. He just needs feet on the earth to make sure his work gets done. With God on your side, you do not need to fear your own limitations.

Vision comes before provision. What is *provision*? To provision means to supply with equipment, especially for a journey. You will need help and equipment for your journey here on earth, and God is the perfect one to help you with that.

> Write my answer plainly on tablets,
>> so that a runner can carry the correct message to others.
> This vision is for a future time.
>> It describes the end, and it will be fulfilled.
> If it seems slow in coming, wait patiently,
>> for it will surely take place.
> It will not be delayed. (Hab. 2:2–3)

When you get clear about the vision for your life, the Bible says to write it down and make it plain. Then have faith! God will come alongside you and provide opportunities for that vision to come to pass in ways you cannot even imagine currently. That is how he works. God loves to blow our minds!

4. Spend some time daydreaming and imagining the possibilities for your life.

Give yourself permission to spend time dreaming. Then, when you have a clear picture in your mind, create a vision board or a visual journal. Look at it and pray over it every single day, and watch what happens. These possibilities will eventually become your realities.

5. Be intentional about teaching your mind to dream big.

Your mind controls your brain.[4] So fill it with positive and joyful information, such as audio messages, books, music, and affirmations that will keep you focused on a more significant potential for your future.

6. Play out the what-ifs in your mind.

While you're dreaming, ask yourself some questions:

What if you could earn a living doing what you love?

What if you used your gifts to help others?

What if you quit your current job to start that business?

What if you asked someone you admire for a quick phone call or a conversation over coffee?

What if you took a big step into your purpose today?

7. Do not share big ideas with small-minded people; it's a waste of time.

People who always expect the worst have little hope in a brighter future. These people are not going to get you where you want to go. Limit your time with anyone who is a negative voice in your head, and seek out people who will encourage you to reach for the stars.

8. Train your tongue.

I believe our thoughts create our future, but our words declare it to the world. Words have tremendous power! Stop complaining and sabotaging your future by speaking negatively. Train yourself to speak positively about your life. After all, "Death and life are in the power of the tongue" (Prov. 18:21 NKJV).

| Key Takeaway

Realizing that anything is possible is the first step in creating a specific vision for your life. Your vision is your *big why*. It's a compelling reason you want to do something. It gives you direction, and it is your desired future. Your vision includes what you believe in (your core values). Having a vision will not only teach you how to be intentional with your life but can also change the course of your life forever.

TWO

Purpose

But I have spared you for a purpose—to show you my power
and to spread my fame throughout the earth.

Exodus 9:16

Notice, in Exodus 9:16, that God doesn't say his purpose is to spread *your* fame. The purpose he has in
store for you is part of the plan to spread his fame,
his glory, and his kingdom. And he wants *you* to be part of
his plan! How amazing and exciting is that?

It is thrilling—until that annoying little devil-voice sweeps
in and says, *Why would the God of the universe want to use
you?* I know, because that is exactly what I thought. And
you know what? I still fight that nagging feeling sometimes.
There have been plenty of days (this past year in fact, while
I was starting a new ministry) I heard that same defeating
statement. I am not going to lie; those days have been hard.
I have questioned myself a million times and, quite frankly,
have wanted to give up. But, deep in my soul, I know God is

building my tenacity and my ability to stick with him through the tough times. So instead of quitting, I think (truthfully, I sometimes yell), *Not today, Satan!* and keep on trucking.

Thankfully, God has given me teachers, books, words, podcasts, and so much more to remind me that he always chooses imperfect people to do his work. Why? Because we are *all* imperfect! It may appear that a person you see doing what you have always dreamed about doing looks like they have it all together. But let me tell you, my friend, they *don't*. They just started with a dream, then worked really, really, really hard. If they were smart, they prayed and surrendered a lot too. I can promise you there are still moments when they think, *Who am I to be doing this?*, especially if they are out working for God. The devil hates people like that.

Purpose is something you uncover. Whether you realize it or not, you are being guided toward your purpose every single day. But for you to see this, you must look through God's lens. This means paying attention to the little ways in which God is working in your life. God will use any means he can to align your path to the purpose he has intended for you.

When you know what your purpose is, you can plan ahead and start each day with that in mind. Purpose shapes how you think, how you spend your time, and how you do life. Your life purpose is not your job or your role. Positions and roles are vehicles through which you deliver your purpose.

Your life's purpose comes from within. It was planted inside of you as part of God's plan for his kingdom before you were even born!

Sarah Jakes Roberts says,

You do not choose purpose. Purpose chooses you. When something on the inside of you connects with what's happening outside of you, it is a sign that a portion of your life is a part of the solution. The first step of fulfilling your purpose is allowing yourself to have one. . . . The first thing to understand about purpose is that it will always be rooted in service toward the betterment of humanity.[1]

I believe this, because I believe God had our purpose intended for us before we were even born. He formed each of us in our mother's womb with the exact personality, set of gifts, insights, and talents we would need to see our purpose through. His plan was perfect; we have just lost our focus due to all the distractions in our way.

Friends, I want to tell you that there is no more excellent feeling in the entire universe than waking up each day knowing you are living your God-given purpose. Not only does it allow you to share your God-implanted gifts and talents but, when you are truly aligned with God's will for your life, your purpose will help other people. Deep down, who doesn't want to help make the world a better place? Not to mention this is the number one reason people are remembered after they leave this earth: not for what they had but for what they did! I know it sounds cliché, but deciding how you want to be remembered and then working backward is a great way to live.

Consistent study of God's Word is vital for staying focused on your purpose. I highly recommend that you commit right now to how much time you will spend in God's Word each day. Not only will it give you the wisdom and insight you need for pursuing your purpose but help you stay on course when the journey gets bumpy. It will help you handle stressful situations and lift you up when you are down.

God-Given Potential

What if you currently have no idea what your purpose is? First of all, you are not alone. Each person comes to the realization of their purpose in different ways and in different amounts of time. Shortly I will give you some action steps that may speed up this process, but in the meantime, know that your purpose will have something to do with serving others and making a positive impact in this world. It will be something God needs you to do for him. John Maxwell says,

> Everyone faces difficulty when working toward a dream. And if someone fails, he can make excuses for what went wrong, how the unexpected happened, how someone let him down, how circumstances worked against him. But the reality is that the external things do not stop people. Those who achieve their dreams don't have an easier path than those who do not. They just have a different internal attitude about the journey.[2]

Even if you cannot see your purpose clearly now, do not assume you don't have one. Every person on this earth was birthed out of purpose. Every single one—and that includes you. This truth is not just for the people who are already living out their mission. It is not just for the famous people you watch on social media doing what you dream of doing. *It is for you.* God needs you to carry out the plans he has in store for you. If you don't fulfill your specific purpose, who will?

Jason was not only addicted to drugs but was a drug dealer. His family was devastated and worried about him. His brother constantly brought the Word to him, but Jason didn't give it much attention. His mom kept praying. Years went by, until one day his choices had dragged him downhill until he was on the edge of losing his home, his wife, and his family. He finally decided to check himself into rehab. That night he hit his knees and prayed to God to save him. By the morning his drug addiction was completely wiped clean from his body, with no withdrawal! He was able to return home after his treatment and start a better life.

One day he noticed a bunch of neighborhood kids hanging out near his driveway. He started chatting with them. At the time Jason had no idea what God's purpose was for his life. These chats led to Jason and his wife taking those kids on a camping trip. Fast-forward to today, and Jason is now a pastor at his own church with a growing youth ministry that picks kids up off the streets every Saturday night, feeds them, gives them a message and a time of worship, and then takes them home.

God had a divine purpose for Jason's life all along, but until Jason could clear the clutter caused by addiction, he could not experience it. He was lost and broken . . . but God.

■ ■ ■ ■ ■

You don't have to say the perfect prayers or understand everything. You just have to start with a simple statement like this: "Lord, I ask that your will be done in my life." If you say that prayer every day, I promise you cannot go wrong.

And the Holy Spirit helps us in our weakness. For example, we don't know what God wants us to pray for. But the Holy Spirit prays for us with groanings that cannot be expressed in words. And the Father who knows all hearts knows what the Spirit is saying, for the Spirit pleads for us believers in harmony with God's own will. And we know that God causes everything to work together for the good of those who love God and are called according to his purpose for them. For God knew his people in advance, and he chose them to become like his Son, so that his Son would be the firstborn among many brothers and sisters. (Rom. 8:26–29)

Put your trust in God, because he works *everything* for your good. That doesn't mean you get a perfect life; evil is still working against him. But he can even use that. Note that God is not working to necessarily make you happy all the time; he is fulfilling *his* purpose through you. That is why he brought you to this earth, in hopes that you would achieve that purpose before he brings you back to him.

The Path to Purpose

So, are you ready to find and conquer your purpose? I am so excited for you! Here are some steps you will find helpful when trying to figure out what your purpose is or how to pursue one God has already placed on your heart. The truth is God already knows what your purpose is because it was part of his plan for your life from the beginning of time. He wants *you* to awaken to it so that you can be a blessing to others and, in turn, glorify him! We are not owners of anything, even our purpose, but rather are stewards of everything.

1. Daydream.

As I mentioned in the previous chapter, we all need a little more daydreaming in our lives. Stop right now, close your eyes for five minutes, and imagine. If you could spend more time doing something, what would it be?

2. Spend time with God.

I truly believe God has all the answers for us, and if we spend some time with him, we can uncover our purpose. Time in the Word, time in prayer, and time just listening for the voice of God can really make a difference if you are searching for your purpose.

3. Read, read, and read some more.

It is incredible how much we can learn just by reading. I am a huge reader, and I am always in the middle of one to three books at a time. I have kept a list of books I have read for years on my computer. I also rate them, to help me remember what authors I've enjoyed when I need a new book. These days, I mostly read nonfiction because I am in a learn, learn, learn frame of mind!

4. Think of podcasts and videos as your continuing education.

We are blessed to live during a time when we can find information about almost anything in the world with a click of a button. My advice is to take advantage of this. I listen to podcasts or videos almost every single day. They are a great way to get an inside peek at how others are living and have succeeded, which is excellent for inspiration. For example, on my podcast, *The 29 Minute Mom*, guests share inspiration, motivation, and education that can help moms live their best lives.[3]

5. Ask those closest to you what you are good at.

Sometimes others recognize our gifts more easily than we do. Ask others what they think you are good at. Have they learned something from you? Have you helped them somehow in the past?

6. Get out and try new things.

It is hard to know what you are truly passionate about if you don't try new things. Decide what you want to try, and then go do it. Maybe you can sign up for a new class on the topic. If you don't like it, try something else. Then do it again and again and again. The power of life is in your decisions, not in your condition. You get to decide; you get to choose the life you want to have!

■ ■ ■ ■ ■

There is power with Jesus on your side. Hopefully there will be a time in your life when a light bulb goes off, and you realize deep in your soul what your purpose is. That is the perfect time to go to God and pray:

Lord, is this your will? If not, then please show me what your will for my life is. And if it is, Lord, I ask you to come alongside me and show me the way. Teach me, Lord. I put my trust and hope in you. Please use me to make the world a better place. In Jesus's name, amen.

Key Takeaway

Your life's purpose comes from within. It was planted inside you as part of God's plan for his kingdom before you were even born!

| THREE |

Possessions

Don't store up treasures here on earth, where moths eat them
and rust destroys them, and where thieves break in and steal.
. . . Wherever your treasure is, there the desires of your heart
will also be.

Matthew 6:19, 21

When Desiree was a little girl, she played Barbies
in her room constantly. She loved setting up her
Barbie dream house with furniture, organizing
the clothes, accessories, and handbags in her carrying case,
and pushing Barbie around in her convertible. What Desiree
loved most was fantasizing about living this kind of life when
she was grown up. She couldn't wait until she was an adult
living in her own mansion by the beach, with a closet full of
designer clothes and accessories, married to her handsome
"Ken" and driving around with the top down. Of course,
she would have other vehicles in her driveway, as well as her

own private plane, RV, and yacht. Just the thought of it made her feel joyful.

See, though Desiree was only a young girl, she had already been taught by society that possessions were extremely important. They made you feel rich, powerful, and well-liked. She was bombarded by images proving this on magazine covers, in books, and on the TV shows her mom would watch like *All My Children*, *General Hospital*, and *Dallas*. The women in these shows were not only thin and beautiful, but were rich and had homes filled with beautiful things. She wanted to be just like them when she grew up.

I don't believe that this passage from Matthew 6 is saying we shouldn't love anything here on earth, but I do think it is telling us to be careful about what we treasure. We should be cautious of putting too much emphasis on our possessions. Our biggest treasure should be our relationship with God.

Do you find that your material possessions affect how you feel about yourself and how you live your life? Do you find yourself longing for that trendy handbag, those new sneakers, or the latest cooking appliance that will definitely be the one to make your life easier?

I want you to know there is a bigger calling for your life than how many things you can accrue. Yes, we are here to collect—but not clothes, appliances, documents, or money. We are to gather wisdom, memories, positive character traits, ways to do God's work, love, and so much more. None of which has anything to do with how many things are in our homes.

I have had the experience of emptying countless homes. Clients have hired me to do this for them when a loved one has passed away. I have also done this for both of my grandparents' homes. It is a crazy experience, to be honest with you. It can be very overwhelming. But each time I have done this, the same thoughts go through my head. I imagine how many hours that person worked to obtain their possessions and how many hours they spent cleaning, rearranging, and moving things in and out. And yet even though they gave so much of their lives to these things, here the stuff remains on earth when they are gone. What is it all for? My sincere prayer is that it was all worth it, and that these material items gave them joy while they lived with them. But in the end, we all leave here empty-handed.

What is in our hearts and how we contribute to making the world a better place are what matter to God. After all, someday all your possessions will be gone, and at that point, what will be left of your time here on earth? How will people remember you? Trust me, you will not be remembered for how many pairs of shoes you owned (unless maybe if you are Jackie O)! Rather, as the Bible says,

> Let us strip off every weight that slows us down, especially the sin that so easily trips us up. And let us run with endurance the race God has set before us. (Heb. 12:1)

A Different Kind of S.T.E.M.

Imagine your home. Think about the colors of the walls, the layout of the furniture, and the trinkets all around. Now, think about how you feel about your space.

Is your home a true external reflection of who you are on the inside?

Does your mind feel as cluttered as your home looks? What are the things you own costing you?

Have you ever realized that everything you own or bring into your home uses up some amount of Space, Time, Energy, and/or Money? Think about it. We only have so much S.T.E.M. in our lives. I think it is super important that we become intentional with how we spend our S.T.E.M.

The next time you feel the urge to buy a bigger house, ask yourself, *How much S.T.E.M. am I willing to give up?*

Are you OK with spending more time and energy cleaning a bigger house? Do you want to spend the money it costs to obtain and maintain a larger home? Are you willing to take away time, energy, and money from other areas of your life to own this type of home?

Seriously, we are all so quick to look at the pros of getting what we want. But sometimes we need to stop and consider the cons too.

While I was reading Jen Hatmaker's book *7: An Experimental Mutiny against Excess*, this statement got me thinking: "Clothes used to define me when my genuine identity was fuzzy. When I didn't know who I was or what I was here for, I dressed like someone who did."[1] I wonder how many other people can relate to this? Can you?

In Mark 10:21, Jesus tells a rich young man: "Go and sell all your possessions and give the money to the poor, and you will have treasure in heaven. Then come, follow me."

What would you say if God asked you to sell your possessions, but with a guarantee that you would spend eternity in heaven with him? Would you do it? The funny thing is that I don't think God even wants us to sell everything we own.

But I do believe he wants us to have an open hand. I think he wants us to bless people whenever we can. (We will dive deeper into that in a later chapter.)

Take Stock

There is a direct connection between outer order and inner calm.[2] If you don't believe me, stare at a cluttered area of your home for ten minutes. Take note of how it makes you feel. Do you feel stressed, overwhelmed, embarrassed, or tired? Now, declutter and organize that space, then stare at it for another ten minutes. Again, check in with your emotions. I guarantee that you now feel better than you did before. You now probably feel energized, happy, calm, or even giddy. *That* is why it is so important to be intentional about your possessions.

> This is what the LORD of Heaven's Armies says: Look at what's happening to you! You have planted much but harvest little. You eat but are not satisfied. You drink but are still thirsty. You put on clothes but cannot keep warm. Your wages disappear as though you were putting them in pockets filled with holes! (Hag. 1:5–6)

This Scripture reminds me of what I like to call the "five-minute high" principle: the feeling of joy or contentment you get when you purchase something. How many times have you gone into Target, bought something, and got in your car feeling elated? On your drive home, you can hardly wait to get that object into your house and put it somewhere. Oh, the joy you are feeling! You know this item will make you so happy.

Fast-forward a month, six months, a year, maybe even more. Is that object still giving you joy every time you pass by it? Maybe, and if that is the case, you made a smart purchase. But I would bet this is not the case 90 percent of the time. You may not even remember which items in your house made you feel that way to begin with.

Here are two ways to assess your relationship with material possessions.

1. Freeze your spending.

If you want to get really radical, I recommend trying a spending freeze. A spending freeze means you stop buying nonessentials for a while. It can be very helpful when you are working on getting your home organized. Initially, it will make your life easier, because buying more adds to the work! It will also reboot your mind so you can start viewing your possessions differently. If you are feeling extra overwhelmed by clutter, the best thing you can do is get organized and reduce the number of items in your home.

2. Engage your marketing awareness.

Did you know that we see about five thousand marketing messages per day? The purpose of these messages is to get us to want more and think we need more. The people behind these messages know how to do this well. It is crucial that we become aware of how these messages affect us. Most of them are lies: we don't *need* more. Most products will not improve our lives.

■ ■ ■ ■ ■

Many times, our desire for more or better possessions is really a longing to fill an empty place inside of us. In the

Scripture above, God uses the prophet Haggai to give a message to the people of Jerusalem because they were more worried about making their homes beautiful and gaining things than they were about doing God's work of rebuilding the temple. The harder they worked, the less they had, because they were ignoring their spiritual lives. The same will happen to us. We can work hard to gather more and more stuff, but without God as the center of our lives, we will never stay satisfied. We will always want more and more, because true contentment only comes from a personal relationship with our Creator.

How many times a week do you scroll through Instagram or Facebook or flip through the pages of a magazine, wishing you had what other people have? We all do this to some point, but be careful that you are not coveting. To *covet* is to wish to have the possessions of others. It goes beyond admiring someone else's possessions or thinking, *I would like to have that.* Coveting includes *envy*, or resenting the fact that others have what you don't have. In today's society, we see other people's possessions more than ever. Never before has it been so easy to see inside other people's homes and lives. In fact, social influencers are encouraged to share as much as possible! If you find yourself secretly coveting the people you follow, it may be time to unfollow them, or at least put your phone down.

As a professional organizer, I am privileged to be able to visit many homes and get an intimate view of the lives of my clients. Often I get to know these people so well that we become friends. They lean on me for guidance, accountability, systems, and resources. Many times I end up becoming their biggest cheerleader.

There have been countless times when I've gotten a call from a new client that led me to a beautiful home, with a perfectly manicured yard and a row of really nice cars in the driveway. When I pull into the driveway, I notice that from the outside anyone would think this person was living the "perfect American dream"—only to meet an overwhelmed homeowner (usually a woman) when the front door opens.

Dina was one of these women. She had it all: three beautiful children, a huge and gorgeous home in a high-end neighborhood, and a marriage to a successful doctor. She was beautiful, extremely intelligent, and had a medical degree.

However, the woman who opened the door that day differed greatly from the one you might imagine with those credentials. She was overwhelmed, defeated, and severely depressed. She was in the middle of a failing marriage, caring for a child with special needs all alone, and unemployed. Her home was beautiful but a complete disaster, and her inner spiritual life was in an abyss. My heart broke for Dina that first day, but I could see the possibilities for her life.

Dina tried everything to save her marriage. Unfortunately, in the end, she realized things were never going to change, and it was time to move forward and try to find happiness with a bigger vision for her life. She gave up her big house, along with most of her possessions, to start over. She eliminated the clutter of toxic relationships, stuff she did not love, excess weight, debt, and the opinions of others.

Now, after she worked through several years of grieving the loss of her marriage and all that she thought her life was supposed to look like, I am happy to say she has also eliminated the clutter of regret. Not only did she go back to work as a pediatrician but she has since realized her purpose in aligning pediatrics with supporting the needs of children's mental health. Her children have grown into happy, healthy, successful young adults, and she is in love with a Christ-centered man who appreciates who she is and what she stands for. Dina has worked hard on herself, sought counseling, gotten organized, and spent many, many hours rebuilding her relationship with God. She looks better than ever and is so much happier than the woman who opened the door to me that first day.

Dina is where she is today because she was willing to ask for help when she needed it. She was committed to growth. When she cleared the clutter that was distracting her, she realized God had a specific purpose for her life.

True Treasure

Jesus taught that our loyalty should be to things that cannot fade, cannot be stolen or used up, and never wear out. We should not be fascinated with our possessions, lest they possess us. Without God in our lives, everything will become useless, no matter how valuable it seems at first.

God says a lot about possessions in the Bible. He knows material items will never make anyone happy for long, because only he can supply all of our needs. *Idolatry* is making anything more important than God. The people in the Old Testament were warned about worshiping idols. It might be hard for us to understand today why they were so enamored of idols made of stone and wood. But we are struggling with the same thing, just in a different way. Money, success, beauty, and possessions are the idols of today. Do we think these things can give us the same peace and joy God provides? Do we turn to them instead of to God?

I don't know about you, but when God explains what will happen when we obey his commands, his words excite me:

> I will look favorably upon you, making you fertile and multiplying your people. And I will fulfill my covenant with you. You will have such a surplus of crops that you will need to clear out the old grain to make room for the new harvest! (Lev. 26:9–10)

When we are constantly filling ourselves up with things, we are less focused on filling up with God. Remember, lasting joy does not come from stuff.

When we don't know who we are in Christ, we will try to find our identity in the things we own or what we have, such as our job, security, wardrobe, house, car, or relationships. But we only find real contentment, joy, and wealth by developing our spiritual life, not by building a collection of possessions.

Key Takeaway

Everything we own takes up a certain amount of space, time, energy, and money. We only have so much S.T.E.M. in our lives. I think it is super important that we become intentional with how we spend our S.T.E.M.

HOW TO MAKE ROOM

FOUR

Prepare

Be prepared. You're up against far more than you can handle
on your own.

Ephesians 6:13 Message

Preparation is part of God's nature and his plan.
Throughout history, he has worked in the lives of
people, nations, and circumstances to prepare indi-
viduals and groups for his opportunities, his purposes, and
his blessings. We can see this over and over in the Bible.

Preparing yourself for the dream God has given you is an
act of faith. It shows God that you trust him and have faith
that whatever plans he has for you will come to pass. The
word *prepare* means "to make ready beforehand for some
purpose, use or activity."[1] There's that little word *purpose*
again!

As I write this book, I am in the middle of preparing
for the vision God has given me for using my organizing

platform for ministry. When God first gave me the vision for a ministry in September 2017, I was caught off-guard a little. Honestly, I had no idea how I was going to pull off such a large vision. But he began placing people, books, and messages in my life that helped me to see that this vision could come to pass with his help.

The next May, friends started mentioning to me that Terri Savelle Foy had been discussing my series, Organize Now!, on her television show and podcast. This was really exciting for me, because I had recently started following Terri in my quest to further my knowledge about declaring affirmations over my vision. I reached out to Terri, and after a series of animated emails, we planned to meet face-to-face at the Balanced Living Conference in Toronto. That weekend I learned the importance of preparation as an act of anticipation and how to act and speak about things that do not yet appear as though they have already happened. I thank you, Terri, for teaching me that one! Preparing for what God tells us will come to pass shows faith and trust in him.

A couple of days later, I was listening to Cynthia Brazelton preach (I became a huge fan after hearing her speak at the conference). As God so often orchestrates, it was the exact message I needed to hear on that day. Cynthia spoke of the importance of making a decision and deciding to follow God and his purpose for your life, no matter what. Even if you don't know how you are going to pull it off, you need to say yes to God and trust him. That day, I decided to pursue a life of ministry within my role as an organizing expert. Let me tell you that, at that moment, I felt both excited and scared to death. I said out loud, "OK, God, let's do this!"

There is so much you can do to prepare for your purpose. First, you can begin doing the inner work of strengthening your character. I truly believe that the essential part of any dream is not the moment you achieve it but the person you become along the way.

God knows us better than we even know ourselves. After all, he created us. He knows the future, which means he knows who we'll need to be to sustain the dream once it happens. For example, if you are going to put yourself out there in the public eye, you will face criticism. Not everyone will like you or agree with you (and that is OK). So God will want to create in you a tough skin, an open heart, and a boldness to stand firm in the storm of controversy. God will always build you up to be the person he needs you to be in order to do what he needs you to do.

Simply Begin

You may wonder why you should prepare for something you don't even know will definitely happen. Preparation gets you ready for an opportunity. It frees up space and time in your life. It limits your excuses for not moving forward when the opportunities start knocking. You will know you are ready because you have prepared.

God is giving you small opportunities now to develop you for something more prominent in the future. In John Maxwell's book *Put Your Dream to the Test*, he writes that before you start doing big things, you can still find contentment in doing the right things. No act of kindness is too small to be worth doing.[2] He reminds me of this quote popularly attributed to Saint Francis of Assisi: "Start doing what is necessary; then do what is possible; and suddenly, you are doing the impossible."

Here are some simple steps you can take to start preparing for your dream.

1. Declutter your surroundings.

Many people feel that not having a plan adds to the spontaneity and freedom of life. But when we plan wisely and get our lives in order, we experience more joy, less stress, and a calmness that enables us to show up more for God. This is a great opportunity to take inventory of your life and look for areas that need a little cleanup. Maybe you need to clean up your finances, or you need better time management. Now may be a great time to declutter room by room. If you need an extra dose of inspiration or links to resources, check out my website, www.jenniferfordberry.com. Whatever it is, now is a good time to spend getting your life in order, because once your purpose is discovered it is all you will want to do, trust me!

2. Speak your dream into existence.

Speaking about what you want to see in your life as if it has already happened is the key to manifestation. We release our faith with our words. Come up with a list of affirmations about your life and speak them out loud every single day. One of my favorite ways to do this is to make a list at the beginning of the new year that looks like this: I'll write "2022 was the best year of my life because . . . " at the top of the page. Then I'll write down all the things I want to happen that year as if they have already taken place, such as "*Make Room* became a *New York Times* bestseller."

3. Protect your mind.

I am a true believer that our thoughts can bless or destroy our future. Our thoughts eventually become our reality. For example, you could have a fit body and be the perfect weight for your shape and your height. But if you told yourself every day that you were fat, you would eventually believe it, and in time you would act like you were a fat person (hiding behind clothes that are too big, feeling insecure, and so forth). Therefore it is crucial to learn to control your mind by filling it with motivational and inspirational messages. As the apostle Paul instructs, you should "fix your thoughts on what is true, and honorable, and right, and pure, and lovely, and admirable. Think about things that are excellent and worthy of praise" (Phil. 4:8).

Stay the Course

It is not easy to stay in the space of your dream when you can't yet see it. Trust me, I know! You may have days when you don't feel like preparing for whatever reason. On those days, I tell myself this simple belief: *Why would God bother giving me a vision for my future that he would not see come to pass?* I also remind myself that his timing is not always the same as my timing. But, man, we are impatient humans, right? And then I keep going, putting one foot in front of the other, taking steps of diligence, practicing stewardship, and being bold. If you have a tough day, call someone who will lift you up, email me at organize@jenniferfordberry.com, or pray for the Holy Spirit to give you a fresh dose of energy and encouragement.

The biggest distraction when you are trying to stay on the right path is Satan. He does not want you to succeed if you are working with God, and he will do whatever it takes to distract you. Do not be surprised if, when you begin clearing the physical clutter from your life, Satan distracts you with other tasks or interruptions. He doesn't want you to be prepared. Why? Because when you are prepared, you are powerful!

Do your best to avoid laziness and idleness. It is essential to give yourself time for rest, leisure, and relaxation to maintain balance in your life. But too much is not what you were created for.

In 2 Thessalonians 3, Paul talks about the proper way of living:

> And now, dear brothers and sisters, we give you this command in the name of our Lord Jesus Christ: Stay away from all believers who live idle lives and don't follow the tradition they received from us. For you know that you ought to imitate us. We were not idle when we were with you. . . . Even while we were with you, we gave you this command: "Those unwilling to work will not get to eat."
>
> Yet we hear that some of you are living idle lives, refusing to work and meddling in other people's business. We command such people and urge them in the name of the Lord Jesus Christ to settle down and work to earn their own living. As for the rest of you, dear brothers and sisters, never get tired of doing good. (vv. 6–7, 10–13)

He is very clear that we should make the most of our gifts and spend our time doing all we can to provide for ourselves and our dependents. I love this as a parent, because it reminds me to work hard; my children are watching how I live. So many times clients have said to me, "I don't know how to maintain an organized home because I was never taught this." I truly believe one of our goals as parents is to teach our children how to be responsible, hard-working, and grateful people. How can we do that if we are not an example of this ourselves? The bottom line is, if we rest when we should be resting and work when we should be working, we are living life properly.

Do you remember earlier when I told you about Terri Savelle Foy talking about my book? Well, she had mentioned on her show how she used my book to prepare for the next step she was going to take. She talked about how she went room by room in her house and cleared away clutter she no longer needed. She prepared. Shortly after, she left her father's ministry, moved to a new city, and started her very own ministry called Terri Savelle Foy Ministries in Rockwall, Texas.

■ ■ ■ ■ ■

My house is in excellent order. Everything has a home. I don't keep things I don't love or use. I have to have my house in order because I am easily distracted by clutter, and I know I don't do my best work if I am distracted. But I still wanted to prepare for my new vision of ministry by eliminating any clutter that might distract me. I wanted to do something that showed God I was serious about my decision. So I decided to remove everything in my office that would not aid me in creating this ministry or writing this book. A clean slate! I tossed old business ideas, research from previous books I've written, and presentations that did not align perfectly with my new vision.

I also prepared in other ways. I planted seeds. I tithed to other ministries I felt were working to grow God's kingdom. I spent a lot of time in the Word. I listened to podcasts every single day while I was getting ready for work and while I was in my car. I listened to others who were doing what I wanted to do. I read a *lot*.

Here is the cool part, my friends: the more I "prepared," the more real the vision seemed—and the more vividly I could imagine my dreams coming true.

Key Takeaway

There is so much you can do to prepare for your purpose. First, you can begin doing the inner work of strengthening your character. I truly believe that the essential part of any dream is not the moment you achieve it but the person you become along the way.

FIVE

Plan Your Time

For everything there is a season,
  a time for every activity under heaven.
A time to be born and a time to die.
  A time to plant and a time to harvest.

Ecclesiastes 3:1–2

Before we dive into decluttering your space, we need to talk about one of the main things we all feel like we don't have enough of: time.

I have been married for nineteen years, and we have two teenage children. This is the sixth book I've written. I've spoken all over the country: television shows, radio shows, podcasts, conferences, women's groups, and churches. I work one-on-one with coaching clients about three days per week. I also own and operate a semiannual family consignment event called Mothertime Marketplace where families sell their children's outgrown clutter. I recently launched a brand-new ministry in which we run a Christian teen conference called Blurry and a women's conference called Created Order.

Why am I telling you all of this? Because if I had not learned the skill of successful time management, none of these things would be possible. Without making time to complete each task necessary to achieve each goal, these things would still be dreams stuck in my soul. Truthfully, they could have ended up as what-ifs.

Time is the one thing we are all given equally. Yes, *given*. God has given us this precious gift of time, but he has not guaranteed how long it will last. He has, however, given it reasonably and with intention. You can't buy more nor borrow more. It doesn't matter if you are rich or poor, old or young, educated or not, you still get the same 1,440 minutes each day. The cool thing is you can use this gift to create any life you want.

Using the Gift of Time

How do we engage in successful and productive time management? Let's look at three simple words: *prioritizing*, *planning*, and *productivity*.

Prioritizing

Prioritizing starts with a vision for your life. Like I've mentioned, you must take time to imagine the possibilities for your life. Painting that picture sets the tone for what you want your life to be. Based on that vision, you can set clear goals and aspirations. Once you have established your goals, you will have a clear idea of what your priorities need to be to reach these goals.

So, how do you begin to prioritize? In Elizabeth Gilbert's book *Big Magic*, she says we begin by

[clearing] out whatever obstacles are preventing you from living your most creative life, with the simple understanding that whatever is bad for you is probably also bad for your work. You can lay off the booze a bit in order to have a keener mind. You can nourish healthier relationships in order to keep yourself undistracted by self-invented emotional catastrophes.[1]

Do you know what your obstacles are? First, perhaps, you need to ask yourself, *What are my top priorities right now?*

I love asking this question when I am speaking to an audience. There is always someone who rattles off their priorities like a proud little robot: "Faith, family, work, health, and giving." Then I'll ask, "How many of you live out these priorities each day?" Maybe half of the audience will raise their hands (usually less), but most of the time I see their faces looking perplexed as they think about this question.

Knowing your priorities and living them are two very different things. Priorities aren't just what is important to you; they are focal points of how you want to spend your time. The priorities you have now may only last for six months, or a year, or five years. It just depends on your goals.

The truth is, many of us can easily rattle off our priorities. If you are a parent, your priorities will include your kids. If you are married, they will (hopefully) include your spouse. If you are a Christian, they will include God. If you like to be healthy, they will include exercise.

71

But how often do you go on dates with your spouse? When was the last time you sat down quietly with God? How often do you make time to work out?

I encourage you to spend some time today thinking about the top priorities you want to *live*. Your priorities should be closely related to the habits you want to form in your life. If you *want* a priority to be weight loss, then you are going to develop the habit of working out regularly. Come up with five or ten priorities to focus on for the next six months to a year. What does that vision for your life look like? Write it down (remember chapter 1?).

Here are some ideas to get your sparks flying:

Lose forty pounds.

Sponsor a child.

Improve your relationship with _____.

Read for _____ minutes per day.

Exercise three days a week.

Create a budget and live within it.

Wake up earlier and spend time in the Word.

The options are endless! Post your list where you will see it daily, especially when you are planning out your week. If you want to add power to this, pray over your priorities every single day.

Honoring priorities often requires hard work, but the work is always rewarding because it produces a result you will love. Look closely at your list and come up with five action items you can begin doing this week to help you live your priorities. For example, if you want to spend more time together as a family, start a tradition of a weekly family fun night or make a commitment to eat dinner together around the table every night. You may need to give up some of your current activities to make more time for your priorities. That's OK. No one can do it all. Delegate your low-priority tasks whenever possible so you have time for what really matters to you.

Commit to continuing your personal and spiritual growth. This type of growth produces two results:

1. Your priorities will continue to improve and align with your true beliefs and principles as you discover what those beliefs and principles are.
2. You will become more aware of when you are not living in a way that honors your priorities and values.

Planning

Planning combines your priorities with the twenty-four-hour period of time we've all been given. Said another way, your daily schedule should always reflect your top priorities. For example, if your goal is to lose fifteen pounds, your priorities must include exercise and healthy eating habits. To do this, you will need to make time to exercise and plan out your meals. You have to be *intentional*. Most of us have heard about the Pareto Principle, aka the 80/20 Rule: 80 percent of the results you are trying to achieve will come from 20 percent of your actions. So when you sit down to plan out your day, focus on the tasks that are going to get you to your end result faster.

Productivity

Productivity is about so much more than doing a lot of different things. You can have a full schedule, but that doesn't guarantee you are getting any closer to accomplishing your goals or priorities. There is a difference between being productive and being busy. Busy people know how to fill their calendars with things, but productive people know how to use their time to get stuff done. They create systems and work those systems over and over. They know how to eliminate distractions and stay focused. They know the importance of completing projects in a timely manner so they can move on to the next goal.

Through reading the Bible, we learn that to be productive for God, we must obey his teachings, resist temptation, actively serve and help others, and share our faith. Are you being productive for God? Are you staying on task with your bigger purpose, or are you letting the world distract you every ten minutes?

If you are serious about living your purpose, you are going to need to get serious about planning out your time to be productive. Winging it does not work well. Trust me! As long as you are alive, you will have a to-do list and responsibilities, so you may as well learn the best practices for managing them. The sooner you do so, the sooner you will feel calmer and more in control when you wake up in the morning and start your day.

One key concept for getting organized is that everything you own needs a home. This concept also applies to time management. Even more importantly for time is the fact that it requires one home: you have one place where you store your schedule and map out your days. It doesn't matter if you use a paper planner or the calendar on your phone as long as you are only maintaining one schedule for your life. If you are currently using one calendar for home and another for work, combine them. It is also crucial that your calendar be mobile and with you at all times. Otherwise, you will have to remember to write things down later. I don't know about you, but chances are I will get distracted and forget!

Currently, you may be seriously overwhelmed with all the things you need to get done. You may feel like you do not even have the time to sit down and plan your week, but I'm sure you've experienced the frustration that comes with winging your schedule. When was the last time you were late to work because you didn't think about making lunch until the last minute? You have to take back control of your time instead of letting others and circumstances control it for you. Not only will this help you feel better but it will empower you.

To be successful in living out your purpose, don't confuse activity with productivity. Remember, you can be "busy" and not get much accomplished. We are all "busy," but how are you using your time to be productive?

Read about any successful person living out their purpose, and you will see a common thread: efficient use of time. If you want to be successful at *anything*, you must learn how to manage your time efficiently. Your goals lead to your priorities, which drive your to-do list, which is married to your schedule.

Successful Goals = Priorities + To-Do List + Schedule

Are you pumped up to get really good at managing your time? I sure hope so. Here are some steps you can take to help you manage your time more efficiently.

75

A Practical Path to Planning Your Time

A few years ago I made a huge change in my life: I went from using a paper planner to my phone calendar. I never thought I would do this because I genuinely love paper planners—what organizer doesn't, right? Each year I looked forward to picking out just the right one for me. There was nothing more exciting than that fresh, clean slate when I opened it up. But it was inconvenient if I forgot to bring it with me and someone asked me about a date or tried to make an appointment with me. Plus, all those cross-outs and eraser marks were ugly.

I'll be honest; I wasn't sure I could stick with a digital calendar at first, but after a couple of months, I started loving it. I found it has many benefits:

- You can easily add tasks and move them around.
- The same calendar can sync to your phone and your computer.
- You can view recurring events and appointments from the past.
- You can set recurring tasks easily without writing them out.
- You can sync calendars and share events with your family and friends.
- You can color-code and categorize.
- It is always with you.

Are you ready? Let's begin.

1. Make and organize your to-do list.

Think of your to-do list as your brain dump: a place where you store all your tasks so you don't forget them. The truth is, you will never get to the end of this list. As long as you are alive on this earth, you will have things you need to do. And who knows, we may even need one in heaven!

So, I want to encourage you to embrace your to-do list as a tool that will help you get the most out of the life you have been given. After all, if you have things to do, then you can thank God for the breath you still have. I highly recommend putting your to-do list into a digital format. If you write your to-dos on paper, it will get messy over time, and you will waste time rewriting it over and over.

Once you have created your list, divide your to-dos into categories. You might have a personal list, a work list, and separate lists for specific projects. Categorizing helps you stay focused whenever you set aside time to work on this part of your life. For example, if I carve out two hours to write, I want to pull up the list dedicated to my current writing project and not get distracted by seeing personal to-dos.

Next, prioritizing your tasks will help you to discern what needs to be done first. Often people sit down, look at their to-do list, and have no idea where to begin. If you prioritize, you can quickly see what needs your attention the most. I teach the A, B, C method to help prioritize tasks:

A = needs to get done this week.
B = needs to get done this month.
C = needs to get done whenever you have time.

2. Plan out your days.

Plan out your time as far as you can. The more intentional you are with your time, the more you can get done. Grab your calendar and mark down every appointment that is already scheduled, such as work hours, kids' activities, exercise classes, school hours, travel booked, and so forth. Decide on a time and day each week you will sit down and plan out the next week: for example, Fridays at 4:00 p.m. or Sunday afternoons at 2:00 p.m. Block out this time and treat it just like you would a set appointment with someone else. Sit down and plug in specific times to accomplish the to-dos on your list.

For example: you see on your schedule that this Tuesday you have a sixty-minute window between the time you get out of work and the time you need to be at your daughter's volleyball game. That would be a great time to get three errands done on your list. Then, on your way home, you can make two important phone calls: one to the dentist to set up appointments and one to call that painter and see when they are available. Voila! Five tasks off your list.

3. Create routines.

Once you've planned out your schedule, you will probably notice trends and recurring events. These can help you build regular routines. Routines are formed by habits, so if you don't like your routine, then you need to change your habits. My advice is to fake it until you make it. What I mean is, come up with a routine that will help you live the way you want to live, and then force yourself to live this way for a minimum of twenty-one days. It takes about that long to begin forming a new habit. Sure, there will be plenty of days when you don't feel like living this way, but do it anyway so it becomes comfortable and normal for you. I promise it will be so worth it.

4. Get accountability.

If you want to get serious about making the most of the time you have, you are going to need some accountability. An exact time management system takes serious diligence and self-discipline. I recommend asking one or two people to help keep you accountable to a time management system until it becomes second nature for you. Ask a spouse, friend, or coach to check in with you regularly. Permit them to give you a pep talk or a swift kick in the backside when you need it. I have done this with hundreds of my clients, and because of it I have seen lives transformed as dreams and possibilities become real purpose with passion.

Key Takeaway

Time is the one thing we are all given equally. It is how we *choose* to use this time each and every day that determines whether or not we live an intentional, productive, and fulfilling life.

SIX

Part with Clutter

For God has not given us a spirit of fear and timidity, but of power, love, and self-discipline.

2 Timothy 1:7

When people are overwhelmed by clutter, they are not in the right frame of mind to read a novel-length book to figure out what to do. They are desperate for answers, and they are thinking, *Someone please tell me what to do, and I will do it!* They feel overwhelmed because they want to part with clutter but have no idea where to start or how they are going to make time to get it all done. That is why I wrote my first book in a step-by-step format. The fact that it is still selling well today tells me that a spelled-out plan is exactly what people want.

First of all, what is clutter? I like to say that clutter comes in all shapes and sizes. It can be many things: baggage from relationships, disappointments, failures, debt, excess weight, that negative voice in your head, and most notably *stuff*.

Clutter can be anything that doesn't aid you in living your best life—and it always costs you something.

- Clutter causes you to feel overwhelmed or depressed.
- Clutter robs you of your energy.
- Clutter steals 50 percent of your storage space.
- Clutter makes life harder. You have to look longer, travel farther, and dig deeper to find what you are looking for.
- Clutter takes longer to clean.
- Clutter costs you money. If you can't find what you need, you buy a replacement. Or you may be paying to store your clutter.
- Clutter makes it hard to think straight.
- Clutter may affect how you feel about yourself. You may be self-conscious or feel guilty about your clutter.
- Clutter can affect your relationships. For example, if you feel ashamed of your cluttered house, you may be less likely to invite friends and family for visits.
- Clutter takes away the peace and beauty of a home.[1]

So why is it so crucial for us to part with clutter? I believe clutter in many forms can rob us of the life we have always dreamed about. Satan wants to distract us with clutter to keep us from doing God's will. Don't believe me? How many times have you decided to get up early in the morning so that you could spend time with God only to get distracted by other tasks? Maybe your morning went something like this:

You set the alarm so you could wake up an hour earlier today. You get up and start making a cup of coffee. You notice dirty dishes in the sink, so you start loading the dishwasher while you wait for the coffee to finish brewing. This leads to wiping off the messy countertop and dealing with a stack of papers. You finally sit down with your coffee and your Bible. You inhale deeply and begin to pray, but then you hear footsteps because the kids are already up. You think, OK, I will get them out the door, and then I'll do my devotional. *An hour later, you are hugging the kids goodbye. OK, time for your devotional. But first, you are going to throw a load of laundry in so that it will be washing while you spend time with God. Then you decide to make the beds quickly because you can't concentrate on God with all this mess. The next thing you know it is lunchtime, and you still haven't checked in with God.*

Let's look again at that verse from Hebrews 12:

Let us strip off every weight that slows us down, especially the sin that so easily trips us up. And let us run with endurance the race God has set before us. (v. 1)

Yes, clutter is a real problem. According to an article by Kristen McGrath, a home's main source of clutter comes from:

Sentimental items: 26 percent
Papers: 25 percent
Clothing: 21 percent
Toys/leisure items: 15 percent

83

Books: 7 percent

Electronics: 3 percent

Other: 2 percent[2]

But clutter is not all "stuff." Let's dig into some of the different things that may be cluttering up our lives.

Space Clutter

The first and perhaps most obvious category of clutter is items taking physical space in your home. There are two crucial questions to ask yourself when getting your space organized: *Do I love this? Do I use this?*

Your home is the one place in the entire universe that is just for you and the other people who live there. Why not make it the place that comforts you, inspires you, and just plain makes you happy when you walk in the door? To do this, you must learn to be very intentional about what you bring in.

1. Take it in small sections.

My first suggestion is to break your home into small sections. Go through each section and ask yourself, *What do I love? What do I use?* When you are finished, remove the items you do not want immediately. They most likely will fall into distinct categories:

Trash: items that are broken or of no use to anyone else.

Give away: items that are still in great condition or working order and can be passed on to someone else (more on this in chapter 8).

Sell: items you are willing to take the time to sell in
order to recoup some of the money you spent on
them.

Years ago, as I mentioned earlier, I founded a semiannual
children's consignment sale called Mothertime Marketplace
because I saw the benefit for parents to recycle what their
children had outgrown. I also knew it was an excellent way to
earn money for what children need next! I don't know about
you, but making money always motivates me to part with my
clutter. Every time this sale rolls around, I go through our
house and make a pile of things my kids have outgrown or
our family no longer needs. After the sale, I take the money
earned and put it in their college funds. Also, if you are trying
to pay off debt, one of the easiest and fastest ways you can
start eliminating it is to sell what you no longer love or use!

2. Group like items.

The second step of getting your space organized is to
group like items together. Many times you won't know exactly how much you have of one category unless you pull
that category together. For example, if you are organizing
documents, you'll need to pull paper from all areas of your
home, including the nooks and crannies you have shoved it
into such as drawers, baskets, and cupboards.

Once you have all of the items in a category together,
you can begin the process of sorting and purging. Be honest
about how much you really need or want. Repeat this process
for each of your various categories. Categories that I often
see spread out too far in a home include gift wrap, shoes,
books, linens, games/toys, and office supplies.

Consolidating these categories will make it much easier for you to find what you are looking for when you need it.

3. Find a home for everything.

The final step of any organization project is to make sure that everything you own has a place. All similar things you love or use have a *specific space* in your home. You will know your home is 100 percent organized when every item in it has a designated spot. Yes, items will come out of those spots, but when you are done using them you should be able to put them back quickly and easily. I will give you a tip: if you do not have room to give everything you own a home, you have *too much stuff*.

Mental Clutter

Mental clutter can take a toll on your life and your ability to reach your highest purpose. It can also make it hard to focus for more than a few minutes at a time. As a society, we need to learn how to stop being forgetful, focus, and stop letting distractions send us into a tailspin. Getting organized is one of the best things you can do to relieve stress, worry, and anxiety. Most people's minds are so cluttered they can barely keep the same thought for a consistent sixty seconds.

Mental clutter can make you feel:

- overwhelmed
- fearful
- stressed
- tired

Consider these common culprits of mental clutter. Which do you need to clear from your life?

Worry and Fear

Worry and fear can keep us from making a change in our lives or stepping out in faith toward a new goal. They can paralyze us. Satan loves to use fear to keep us from taking bold steps into what God has called us to do, and he knows it is easy to get us on the worry train. But when we start to get on board, we can remind ourselves to place our trust in our Creator and move away.

Negative Self-Talk

Negative self-talk is like having someone follow you around all day constantly pointing out all of the things that are wrong with you, or like a voicemail in your head that just keeps repeating over and over. It is very distracting and a complete waste of your time and energy. Examples can sound like, *My dreams will never come true. Who am I to have a calling that big on my life? I am not skinny enough, rich enough, bold enough. I need to make everyone happy.*

Perfectionism

If you are waiting for the "perfect time" to do something, you will be waiting for your entire life. The time is *now* to make a change, end a relationship, start a business, follow your heart, or write a book. If not now, then when? My friend, there is never really a perfect time. There will always be questions, doubts, and fears, but stepping out in spite of them is what stretches us and helps us to learn. I wrote my first book between my kids' naps, cooking dinner, and running a little consignment store. My son was a baby and my daughter was a toddler! It was by no means the perfect time, and you have to know this: I had no idea what I was doing. I just started writing, and then whenever I had a spare ten minutes I would write some more (in fact, that is much like I am writing this book now). By the way, it is still not the "perfect" time for me to write. But if I were waiting for that, I would never have finished even one book.

People-Pleasing

The underlying urge to make others happy is not necessarily a bad thing. But when it gets to the point that you are doing so to the detriment of yourself, it becomes a problem. If you are obsessing about making someone else happy or getting them to like you, that is a form of mental clutter.

Relationship Drama

Have you ever gotten into an argument with a friend or family member and replayed the words you spewed at each other over and over in your head? Have you ever wondered why a friend has been distant but haven't addressed the issue face-to-face? These thoughts will surely clutter up your mind (and most likely your spirit too). The best way to clear much of this mental clutter is to have an open and honest conversation with the person you are in relationship with. Many times our assumptions are much worse than reality.

Triggers

Speaking of relationships that have been altered or destroyed, I would like to mention triggers. We all have *triggers*, or things that can push our buttons. Triggers are usually birthed from thoughts—ones we have carried around for a long time. Thoughts that actually have nothing to do with the situation currently taking place but more to do with our perception of the situation. Say you have a disagreement with someone you love, and then it turns into a big issue in your relationship. Something the other person said or did triggered a reaction in you, but it didn't stop there. Now both of you are not just dealing with this particular issue but deep down are also dealing with your pasts that contributed to the issue. Now you are fighting over something much bigger than the original disagreement. The thing to remember is this: do not let your triggers define your perception. Stick to the truth and the facts. Perception is a thief of many good relationships. It is so much better to sit down face-to-face and listen to each other with an open heart. Be vulnerable! At least the truth comes out that way.

Financial Debt

Money concerns can also cause a lot of mental clutter. Fear of not being able to pay your bills or, worse, not being able to feed your family can cause you to spend a lot of time worrying. If you are unhappy in your current job, you may spend a lot of time thinking about how you can get out of it and find a new one. Shopping sprees can give you that quick five-minute high you are in search of, but then you're bombarded with thoughts and feelings of guilt after the money is spent. Taking care of your finances is a great way to reduce mental clutter.

Unfinished Tasks/Lack of Time Management

Unfinished tasks may be the biggest culprit of all for mental clutter. When we do not finish tasks we are responsible for, it hangs over us like a dark cloud. It makes us feel irresponsible and unproductive. Those feelings will cause energy to sap from our bodies. But when we make the time to get our to-dos done, we feel an energy burst. When it comes to time management, implementing a system that works for you is crucial to living a balanced life.

Whatever you identify as the main culprit of your mental clutter, it can be hard to know how to start clearing it—especially if you're already feeling stressed and stretched. Here are some tips to help you begin.

Tips to Help with Mental Clutter

1. Get clear on the vision for your life. Daydream until you come up with a very clear description.

2. Journal. Journaling is a powerful tool that helps us stay clear on what we want to accomplish. You can journal about your thoughts, feelings, and even goals.

3. Make a brain dump. List everything you need to do *and* everything you want to do. This will help free up space in your mind.

4. Come up with a system for organizing and completing tasks that works for you.

5. Give yourself permission to have some downtime. What are your favorite things to do to unwind and relax?

6. Let go of the guilt, whether real or imagined. When guilt stems from something you did wrong, you can apologize or avoid repeating your behavior in the future. But when guilt isn't related to actual

misbehavior, it can be counterproductive. Consider whether your standards for yourself are too unforgiving.

7. Simply decide to choose differently. If you don't like the way your thoughts or your actions make you feel, choose differently, and see if it helps next time.

Relationship Clutter

Throughout my career, I have come to realize that while I don't find it difficult to let go of things, I do have a tough time letting go of people. My attachment to people is something God and I have been working on together. Over the past few years, as my walk with God has become more intense, there have been some relationships in my life that have changed form. I'll be honest; I fought this hard. I wanted to keep these people in my life forever. I tried everything: sit-down talks, letters, cards, text messages, and prayer. But I eventually came to some critical realizations. First, a relationship will not work unless both people are fully committed to it. Second, some relationships only last for a reason or a season, and then it is time to move on (and that's OK).

What exactly does relationship clutter look like? Somewhere there is probably a long list, but here are some simple signs that you have relationship clutter in your life:

- You are in a relationship that continually makes you feel badly about yourself.
- You are playing small around certain people so that you don't make them feel insecure.

91

- You spend time with people who do not celebrate your accomplishments.
- You are in a relationship that sways you away from God more than it encourages you to press toward him.

Let's pause for a moment and think through that last item. Are there relationships in your life that you care about more than God? Are there relationships taking up time that you could use for God? Do you spend too much time worrying about them? Thinking about or solving their problems? Stressing over them?

Are you more persuaded by others' beliefs and opinions instead of pursuing an intimate relationship with God? Your relationship with God is extremely personal. Even you and your best friend will not learn the same lessons from God at the same time.

For example, several years ago, two girlfriends and I had a vision for a women's conference in our area. We brought it up to some other women in our church, and they decided to come on board. We formed a committee that included one of the pastors, and she permitted us to hold the conference in our church building. The first year it was amazing! It was indeed one of the best days of my life. I was so proud of the fact that the women who attended came from all backgrounds, religions, and levels of faith. The second year was equally as great. But by the third year, it felt like the church had taken ownership of the event, something that was never part of our vision. I knew God's original concept was for the conference to be an outreach that was not connected to one specific denomination or building. We wanted women to feel comfortable attending regardless of their home church or religion. We wanted them to come and meet Jesus and not feel judged. During that third conference, I felt strongly that we had allowed the flesh to take over a vision God had placed in our hands. It no longer felt right. I spent weeks praying about what to do, and finally knew the right thing was to walk away. It was an uncomfortable conversation to have with our pastor, but I knew I needed to be obedient to God's call and nobody else.

As You Begin

I know it can be challenging to begin the process of clearing away clutter. Whether you feel overwhelmed, don't want to spend the time, or just can't let go of the stuff, parting with clutter can be an emotional process. But please do not give up because it is challenging or time-consuming. The rewards will be well worth the effort, I promise. I have seen countless people transform their lives and increase their happiness just by removing the clutter that was slowing them down.

Let me offer two pieces of advice as you begin decluttering:

1. Do not keep things out of guilt. For example, if you donate the clothing of someone who has passed away, do not feel guilty. Let their memory live on by giving the clothes to someone who needs them today. You are in no way diminishing your love for that person or your memories of them.
2. Do not live in a mode of "just in case" or "what-if." I have heard many people say they keep things because

of a scenario they have decided *could* happen. For example, "I am going to keep this furniture in case we move to a bigger house and have more room." Live in the home you have now. Don't worry about the what-ifs of the next house.

I remember two distinct things about meeting Laura, my client (and now friend), many years ago. When I walked into her home, the first thing she told me was that she loved being a mom. The second thing she told me was that she needed to learn how to organize her home because nobody ever taught her how to do it.

Laura grew up in a well-known family who lived in a house packed with stuff. Her mother, Illene, whom I also worked with, was addicted to that five-minute high—the act of purchasing unneeded things in order to feel happiness. But many times, after Illene returned home those items would sit in a bag, never to be used.

Since the time I met Laura, she has suffered the loss of her only brother and her mother. Her father had already passed away before we met. These losses left Laura, at age forty-two, and one sister as the only remaining members of their immediate family. Due to these deaths, Laura inherited Illene's belongings as well as many of her brother's things, much of which was moved into her house. At first, Laura felt like she needed to keep all of these things as a way of hanging on to the family she loved so much. But it was a huge responsibility, and it consumed much of Laura's space, time, and energy. During her time of grieving, it was important to let the things stay. But as Laura began to heal, she was able to see these items for what they were.

I am so proud of Laura. She learned how to separate herself from her stuff and how to decipher which of her things added value to her life and which didn't. Laura has worked on letting go of the guilt she felt when parting with her family's possessions. She now knows that passing them on to others does not diminish her love for her family or the memories she has. Her home is now cozy, clean, and manageable, and she has more time to spend with her children and her husband, which is her number one priority. Laura has learned the greatest lesson of her life: life is short, and time together is what truly matters, much more than stuff.

Laura's family is very typical of many I have worked with over the years. They have everything they could ever want, yet they feel overwhelmed. Their stuff does not bring them joy. The lack of space, time, and energy causes them stress, and after a while the material things begin to suffocate them because there is just *too much*.

Remember, decluttering is the process of deciding what is most important to you and then clearing away the less important. It can help you get down to what matters most, both physically and spiritually. As the apostle Paul told young Timothy, "Yet true godliness with contentment is itself great wealth. After all, we brought nothing with us when we came into the world, and we can't take anything with us when we leave it" (1 Tim. 6:6–7).

Isn't that amazing! We know this, but we don't live this way. Why? Perhaps we believe the lies this world tells us, the lies that marketing companies get paid big money to get us to buy into: *You need this. If you buy this, you will be more important, more influential, skinnier, healthier, more organized, more respected, and you will save time.* We believe

95

the "he who has the most toys wins" mentality more than we believe what God tells us.

Why is it that we can't take anything with us when we leave this earth? I believe it is because nothing is ours to begin with. It all belongs to God. He wants us to leave it here for the next generation, and the next after that.

The process of parting with clutter is not an overnight event. It is a project that needs to be broken down into specific steps. My prayer for you is that you can enjoy this process and not get bogged down by the work. Many times people run out of steam quickly because they are trying to rush through it. But anything worth doing takes time, patience, and perseverance.

You can do this! I believe in you, and I am excited for you to reap the benefits of getting your home in order. Here are three steps you can take to get started.

1. Create a plan.

The first thing you need is an action plan. Writing out a plan for decluttering will help you feel in control again. Start by making a master list of each space in your home that needs decluttering. For example:

Kitchen

Mudroom

Living room

Master bedroom closet

Master bathroom

Kids' bedrooms

Kids' bathroom

Office

If the room has a lot of clutter, break the room up into zones. For example, the kitchen could be broken up into surfaces, cabinets, drawers, pantry, refrigerator, and so forth.

2. Schedule time to declutter.

This process may take a while, so be OK with baby steps. Focus on one area at a time, completing that one area before moving on to the next. After you make your list, schedule appointments in your planner for each area on the list. If you plan one hour, set an alarm for yourself. When the alarm goes off, give yourself credit for completing the task at hand and move on to something else. Over time, these individual tasks will add up to big projects completed.

3. Get help.

If you are still finding it challenging to begin, ask for help. Maybe you have a friend or family member who is good at organizing. If not, hire a professional organizer. We are expert clutter cutters. I am part of a fantastic network called Faithful Organizers. To see if there is a member of this group in your area, go to www.faithfulorganizers.com.

Finally, get serious about clearing away any clutter that may be coming between you and God. This process will show him you are ready to be used by him for more. And the next time you are walking through Target, tell yourself, *I have all I need and more.*

Key Takeaway

Parting with clutter is the process of deciding what is no longer serving you well and then removing it in order to make room for what will serve you better. It is a project that needs to be broken down into specific steps.

SEVEN

Practice Stewardship

The earth is the LORD's, and everything in it.
The world and all its people belong to him.

Psalm 24:1

Unfortunately, most of us only hear about stewardship during church services that are focused on budgets and building programs. But stewardship goes so much further than that. The Bible says we are to be stewards of this world. First Peter 4:10 says, "As each one has received a gift, minister it to one another, as good stewards of the manifold grace of God" (NKJV). This means we are responsible for managing what God has given us. He has put so much into our hands! Most importantly, he has placed his trust in us.

Mike Richards does a really great job of explaining the idea behind stewardship:

A key to understanding the connection between faith and stuff lies in the distinction between being an *owner* and being a *manager*. The idea of *ownership* is rooted deeply in our culture and society. This is evident even in very young children [and we] carry the right of ownership into adolescence and adulthood as we prioritize our time and finances to purchase more stuff. . . . This ownership mentality is not corresponding to faith in Christ. Growing faith in Christ cannot take place separate from the material reality in which we live. The more we understand Jesus Christ as our Savior, the looser our grip will be on material possessions, or rather, the looser the grip material possessions will have on us.[1]

We need to allow God to move us from a mentality of ownership to one of management. Understanding material items from this new perspective changes everything. As I allow Christ to take his rightful place of ownership in my life, I not only sign over my spiritual life to him but also the physical and material aspects of my life. This means I move from being an owner to being a manager. As a manager, or *steward*, I start to ask, "What does God want me to do with this?" and "How would he want me to treat this?" Instead of holding onto my stuff like a toddler, I look for ways to use, share, and invest what he has entrusted to me for his glory, his purposes, and his kingdom.

Where Do You Stand?

Stewardship, to me, is showing God I am grateful for the things he has already given me by being responsible, capable, and trustworthy with what he puts into my hands. Being a good steward also shows God I can handle more. Have you considered whether you are being a good steward in your life? Here are some questions that can get you thinking about the answer:

Are your clothes clean and put away, or are they lying in a pile at the bottom of your closet?

Do you manage your meals and grocery shopping efficiently, or do you waste food every week by letting it go stale or rotten before you can eat it?

Are you having a hard time maintaining your small home while praying God will bless you with a larger one?

Do you keep that car you wanted clean, or do you allow yourself and your family to eat in it, leave garbage in it, or rarely wash it?

For we will all stand before God's judgment seat. His Word tells us, "'As surely as I live,' says the LORD, 'every knee will bend to me, and every tongue will declare allegiance to God.' Yes, each of us will give a personal account to God" (Rom. 14:11–12).

As we stand at the end of our lives, facing God in heaven, we will be asked to give an account for how we spent our time on earth. In that moment, he will not want to hear a list of excuses.

"I didn't have the time to do this or take responsibility for that."

"I wasn't sure what I was supposed to do."

"My children and my spouse were distracting me too much."

"I didn't like it."

No, that surely won't cut it. God will merely want to know what we did with what he gave us. Did we complain about the work, or did we practice gratitude? Did we love with all we had, or did we hold long grudges? Were we lazy, or did we work hard every day practicing stewardship?

These are the types of questions that come to mind when I think of the most important conversation I will ever have! If I live my life to the best of my ability, it would be unbelievably rewarding to hear something that goes like this: "Well done, my good and faithful servant. You have been faithful in handling this small amount, so now I will give you many more responsibilities. Let's celebrate together!" (Matt. 25:23).

Can you imagine God saying these words to you? Personally, I can't fathom anything more exciting. The amount of satisfaction and pride I would feel would be exhilarating. When we think of all Christ has given up for us, we should be able to give it our best shot here on earth. After all, this life we have been given is a precious gift, one that should be treated with high intention and responsibility.

> Work willingly at whatever you do, as though you were working for the Lord rather than for people. Remember that the Lord will give you an inheritance as your reward, and that the Master you are serving is Christ. (Col. 3:23–24)

You can start today by showing God you are capable of handling more by taking care of what you already have. If you have been given a family, you are responsible in his eyes for leading them well. If you have been given a home, you are responsible for keeping it clean, doing the repairs, and opening your doors to others in need. If you have been given money, God asks you to share a portion of it with others, save a portion, and spend wisely. Several years ago, my husband and I studied through Dave Ramsey's Financial Peace University curriculum.[2] I love what Dave teaches. I highly encourage you to look up Dave's "Seven Baby Steps" for getting out of debt; trust me, it works! If you apply the 80/10/10 principle to your money, you won't go wrong. Spend 80 percent, save 10 percent, and give 10 percent away.

Where to Go from Here

Several years ago, I was walking on the beach with an old friend whom I hadn't seen in many years. I had always considered her a spiritual mentor and had learned so much from her when I was in my twenties. We were catching up, chatting about life. She was in the middle of a move and complained to me about all the work it was to pack up everything from their old house and unpack in the new house. She was in a terrible mood, even though it was the first time she and I had been together in ten years! I asked her why she was moving. She went on to explain that she and her husband had gotten into some financial trouble. She had prayed and asked God to help them get out of it. She was amazed when the perfect townhouse became available, and they sold their existing house for more than the selling price! The amount of money was exactly what they needed to get out of debt and relieve a lot of stress in their lives. At that moment, I stopped in my beach tracks and asked, "Why are you complaining about the exact thing that you asked God to give you?" She looked confused at first. I said, "God was gracious enough to answer your prayers, and now all you can do is complain that there is some work involved? Obviously, if you ask for a new house, you should expect to have to pack up and move!"

We all have to be very careful about complaining about the responsibility that comes with something we prayed for. One of the most significant components of stewardship is gratitude. God loves to bless us. But he likes it even more when we are grateful for what we receive!

You are the manager of everything God has blessed you with. Now, some of you may be thinking, *How did God bless me with this home? I worked hard and earned money to pay for it.* But have you ever thought of it this way? The right home for your family went on the market at just the right time. God helped you get the job you needed to help pay for that home. Maybe he put the right people in your path or helped you stay calm during your interview.

Sometimes we miss all the ways God has helped us get to where we are today: the opportunities he aligned for us, the people he put in our path, the grace he bestowed upon us at just the perfect time—*his* perfect time, not our own.

When God blesses us with money, opportunities, or things, we have to be careful not to use them to impress others but to bless others. When we are good stewards, we will be given even more, because we are showing God we can be trusted with what we already have.

Practicing stewardship is not always easy or convenient, but it is imperative if we are to live on purpose. Here are some helpful steps you can take to become a better steward.

1. Be grateful for what you have now.

If you are not already doing so, I encourage you to look at all your belongings as blessings from God. The Bible says everything happens in his perfect timing. This would mean that there are no coincidences. Stop right now and thank God for all the blessings he has given you. Look around and feel the gratitude! Say a prayer of thanks for the possessions you already have.

2. Don't be wasteful; use up what you have.

As a professional organizer, I've witnessed a massive amount of overconsumption in many of the homes I've visited. It is common for me to see a large category of products, such as makeup, books, clothes, foods, supplements, shoes, and more. If you already have something in your home, you can comfortably live without buying more. I encourage you to start trying to use up what you have. Not only will you save on your grocery bill that month, for example, but you will also waste less. Part of being a good steward is knowing what you have and when you need more.

3. Plan your financial future.

Create a spreadsheet of all of your debts. Write down what you owe on each and a specific date for that debt to be paid. Then write down your goals for saving. Pray and ask God to show you ways you can make money and save money. You can find a spreadsheet like this on my website if you need help: https://jenniferfordberry.com/shop/debt-reduction-worksheet/.

4. Sow seed.

I once heard Terri Savelle Foy say, "While we tend to be need-minded, God is seed-minded." I love that. When you are ready to get serious about increasing your finances, you will want to sow seeds. A "seed" or faith offering is money given in faith that God will multiply it and return it to the giver. I encourage you to do some research on the idea of sowing and reaping. The Bible goes into great detail on this topic. For example,

> Don't be misled—you cannot mock the justice of God. You will always harvest what you plant. Those who live only to satisfy their own sinful nature will harvest decay and death from that sinful nature. But those who live to please the Spirit will harvest everlasting life from the Spirit. (Gal. 6:7–8)

> Remember this—a farmer who plants only a few seeds will get a small crop. But the one who plants generously will get a generous crop. You must each decide in your heart how much to give. And don't give reluctantly or in response to pressure. "For God loves a person who gives cheerfully." And God will generously provide all you need. Then you will always have everything you need and plenty left over to share with others. (2 Cor. 9:6–8)

> When you give to someone in need, don't do as the hypocrites do—blowing trumpets in the synagogues and streets to call attention to their acts of charity! I tell you the truth, they have received all the reward they will ever get. But when you give to someone in need, don't let your left hand know what your right hand is doing. Give your gifts in private, and your Father, who sees everything, will reward you. (Matt. 6:2–4)

In other words, you get as much or as little as you give. If you look at your possessions as blessings from God with the attitude that you are taking care of his property, then you will make what you have more available to others.

Key Takeaway

Learning to look at all of your possessions as blessings from God will help you to appreciate the responsibility that goes along with being blessed. Good stewardship shows God that you appreciate what he has bestowed upon you and that you are willing to take proper care of it.

| EIGHT |

Privileged Giving

Give, and you will receive. Your gift will return to you in full—pressed down, shaken together to make room for more, running over, and poured into your lap. The amount you give will determine the amount you get back.

Luke 6:38

In Luke 6, Jesus clearly tells us that if we have more than we need of anything, we should give to someone who has a greater need. Now, at first, you may feel a little clingy to your things. This stuff makes you happy or makes you feel important—but by faith, we have to believe Jesus. He is not saying this to rob us or punish us; he is saying it to bless us more. This is how he works, amen! I believe his Word is true: as I give, I will receive. Holy Spirit, please encourage us all to have the courage to give more than feels comfortable at first.

There is an abundance of "stuff" in this world going to waste. Whether it is going to a dumpster or sitting in your home unused and unloved, it is being wasted if it is not in the hands of those who need it most. If you are living in a situation where you have the ability to share your time, money, possessions, or resources, you are blessed to be able to practice privileged giving.

Don't feel privileged? Here are some current statistics that may make you think differently about how privileged you are:

More than one in ten people on the planet—844 million—lack basic drinking water access.

Every day, more than eight hundred children under age five die from diarrhea attributed to poor water and sanitation.

There are 2.3 billion people living without access to basic sanitation.

To date, 892 million people practice open defecation.[1]

Since everything we possess comes directly or indirectly from God and ultimately belongs to him, we should freely give a portion to him and a portion to those in need. We all need to do our share in taking care of others in this world.

In 2 Corinthians 9, Paul is talking to the Corinthians about giving, and I think he explains it beautifully:

Remember this—a farmer who plants only a few seeds will get a small crop. But the one who plants generously will get a generous crop. You must each decide in your heart how much to give. And don't give reluctantly or in response to pressure. "For God loves a person who gives cheerfully." And

God will generously provide all you need. Then you will always have everything you need and plenty left over to share with others. As the Scriptures say,

> "They share freely and give generously to the poor.
> Their good deeds will be remembered forever."

For God is the one who provides seed for the farmer and then bread to eat. In the same way, he will provide and increase your resources and then produce a great harvest of generosity in you. (vv. 6–10)

In the Bible, God asks us all to be joyful givers, just like he is. Wealth and possessions mean nothing when it comes to getting into heaven; this is only possible with God. The more you have, the more time, energy, and money it takes to take care of those possessions. If you want to make it easier to keep your home neat and tidy, the simplest thing you can do is give, give, and give some more! Not only will you be a blessing to others and yourself but you will get back some of your time, energy, and money.

How do we decide how much is right for us to give? In the Old Testament, God directs his chosen people to *tithe*, or to give 10 percent of their annual earnings, produce, or possessions, but I think the apostle Paul can also help us answer this question: "Whatever you give is acceptable if you give it eagerly. And give according to what you have, not what you don't have" (2 Cor. 8:12).

Paul then goes on to share several principles to follow:

1. Each person should follow through on their promises.
2. Each person should give as much as they are able.

111

3. Each person must make up their own mind how much to give.

4. Each person should give in proportion to what God has given them.

If you feel like you don't have extra money to give, you are to give what you can. Giving is not just about money. You can also give your time, your possessions, and your service.

Some Practical Examples

Here are some practical ways you may be able to give, starting today (please note you should always call your local non-profits first, and ask what they are in need of).

Animal Shelters

Foster a pet

Donate soft items:

- stuffed animals
- used blankets, pillows, and towels

Donate your pet's gently used items:

- leashes and collars
- bowls
- toys
- grooming tools

Volunteer to walk dogs or clean

Donate cleaning supplies:

- paper towels
- trash bags

- toilet paper
- old newspapers
- hand sanitizer

Domestic Violence Programs

Donate cash

Make an in-kind contribution. These most-needed items are frequently in short supply and make the largest impact:

- laundry detergent
- toiletries (even travel-size ones)
- makeup
- feminine hygiene products
- diapers and baby formula
- gift cards
- housewares (cutlery, sheets, blankets, pillows, toasters, coffee makers, and towels)
- school supplies
- clothing (everything from pajamas to dress clothes for appearing in court)

Food Banks

Donate. The most common needs for food banks include:

- peanut butter
- canned soup/stew
- canned fruit
- canned vegetables

- canned fish
- canned beans
- dried pasta
- brown rice

Volunteer your time:
- help serve food
- pack up and deliver meals

Local Churches

Donate. Many common items appreciated by churches include:
- office supplies
- craft supplies for kids
- school supplies for childcare services
- cleaning supplies
- paper products

Volunteer your time:
- greet people at the door
- help with the childcare program
- offer your services to other areas that need assistance

Libraries

Donate:
- used books and magazines
- used CDs and DVDs

Volunteer your time for special events or ongoing programming

Habitat for Humanity

Get involved with one of their many building projects

Donate (please note that each Habitat ReStore is unique, and many locations also accept items outside these categories):

- gently used appliances
- furniture
- building materials
- household goods
- dishes
- flooring
- lighting (lamps, chandeliers, ceiling fans, breakers, conduit, connectors, and fuses)
- lumber and trim (minimum six feet long with no nails or paint)
- mirrors that are framed
- tools
- windows and doors

The spirit in which we give is more important to God than the amount we give. God does not want us to give begrudgingly or with a bad attitude. He asks us to give because of our love for others, and for the joy of helping those in need. It is simply the right thing to do. Once we have given, we let it go completely. This doesn't mean secretly thinking, *What if I need this someday?*

God also does not want us to give and then brag about it. Have you ever known a person who continually talks about what they have done for others? It gets really old. You don't need to receive credit here on earth. Your generous heart will be well rewarded in heaven.

Joyful Giving

God wants us to have what we need to care for ourselves and our families without being a burden to others. However, we should be willing to give when God asks us to. This keeps "things" from coming between God and us. It also enables us to use our God-given wealth for good.

To help get into the spirit of giving, think of this process as a form of ministry. God blessed you with things when you needed them. Now, if you no longer love these things or use them, you have an opportunity to bless someone else with them. How cool is that? Focus on the joy of giving and being able to help others.

1. Declutter for those in need.

I have found that most people truly want to give and will give freely—if they know of someone who needs it. When I speak to audiences about decluttering, I am always shocked by how many times someone will raise their hand and ask me if I know of a place that accepts this or that. My response is always the same, and I am going to share it with you now.

If you want to declutter your home, find one or two non-profits in your community that need donations. Now, I am not just talking about Goodwill or the Salvation Army. Almost everybody has heard of those two. I'm talking about the "little guys"—the other organizations in your community that are really in need of items. The exact same items that may be collecting dust in your closets or your basement at this very moment! I highly encourage you to take a few minutes right now to do a Google search and get to know a handful of local nonprofits. Choose the ones that pull at your heartstrings. Not only can you make a huge impact in your community but this is also the best motivation for decluttering your home. Just think of it as your own personal ministry. Who knows, you may even end up getting more involved as you get to know the people who are working behind the organization's name.

(As of this writing I am actively adding nonprofit organizations to the Local Give Directory on my website. Check it out: https://jenniferfordberry.com/local-give/. If you know of an organization that should be listed, I would love to hear about it. Please feel free to email me with its website link and city.)

2. Sow seeds.

Take a moment to consider this Scripture:

Don't be misled—you cannot mock the justice of God. You will always harvest what you plant. Those who live only to satisfy their own sinful nature will harvest decay and death from that sinful nature. But those who live to please the Spirit will harvest everlasting life from the Spirit. (Gal. 6:7–8)

When farmers sow seed, they know exactly why they are doing so. They know what that seed is supposed to produce. What is your seed producing?

If you are wanting and waiting for an answer to prayer, I encourage you to give to another person or organization to show God that you trust him to answer your prayer. I encourage you to sow into others. It is powerful to help someone else along with their purpose or ministry. Then wait and see how God uses this seed.

3. Give gift experiences.

The next time a holiday or birthday rolls around, give the gift of an experience. Do any of us really need more stuff in the house? What we need is more time together! I guarantee that the quality time you spend with someone will be remembered far longer than what you gave them for Christmas in 2005.

Some of my favorite ideas include:

Date cards: create a card and ask someone you love on a date. They can cash it in whenever they are ready.

Membership to the local zoo, a fitness center, an amusement park, a museum, a wine club, an audiobook club, Netflix, Spotify, Hulu, and so on.

Tickets to a concert, a theatrical performance, or even to a destination!

4. Increase your giving capacity.

If we have the Holy Spirit inside us, we will continually learn, grow, and expand our spirit. As believers, we should want to grow in the mature use of all resources, so our giving should expand as well. God can give you this desire and enable you to increase your capacity for giving. Do not miss the opportunity to grow as your walk with him continues.

Key Takeaway

Since everything we possess comes directly or indirectly from God and ultimately belongs to him, we should freely give a portion to him and a portion to those in need. We all need to do our share in taking care of others in this world.

| NINE |

Provide Hospitality

Cheerfully share your home with those who need a meal or a place to stay. God has given each of you a gift from his great variety of spiritual gifts. Use them well to serve one another.

1 Peter 4:9–10

God calls us to hospitality. Hospitality is related to stewardship and giving. Opening your home to share it with others usually requires some cleaning up and preparation. (Turn to the Hospitality Checklist section on page 145 for a little extra help preparing for guests.)

One day my girlfriend and I were sitting around chatting about the fact that hospitality seemed to have become a lost practice. We tallied the number of people who regularly invited us into their homes (besides each other), and our count was shockingly low.

Being a professional organizer has a stereotype attached to it: people often assume I live in a "perfect home" where everything is color-coded, labeled, and Pinterest perfect. But just because I am an organized person doesn't mean things never get messy. I cannot tell you how many times I have gone to a party or visited a friend's home for the first time and they say, "I was so nervous you were coming; I ran around hiding all of our messes!" This makes me feel sad. I don't like it when people are embarrassed about their home. I hate that they think I may judge them. (Trust me: when I am off the clock, your mess is the last thing I am looking at.)

The truth is, we are all afraid of being judged when we invite others into our homes. Even me! When my husband and I first built our house, we gave many tours to friends, family, and even some curious strangers. I knew they wanted to see how I'd organized every little nook and cranny, and I felt like it had to be perfect. I think judgment is one of the main reasons hospitality isn't as prevalent as it once was, along with the fact that we all seem ultra-busy. We are constantly bombarded with images of "perfect" homes online. We often forget that professionals stage these spaces for promoting businesses. They are not a good representation of the average home or the typical busy family.

Where to Begin

Hospitality is defined as "the quality or disposition of receiving and treating guests and strangers in a warm, friendly, generous way."[1] When a girlfriend comes over and admits to you that her marriage is in trouble, or your neighbor pops in to catch up on what your kids have been doing, how do you react? Are you warm and welcoming, able to stop what you are doing? Or are you distracted and maybe even a little annoyed because you were not expecting visitors?

Consider Paul's words in Romans 12:13: "When God's people are in need, be ready to help them. Always be eager to practice hospitality." In the notes section of my study Bible, I found the following explanation about this verse, which I think is beautiful:

> Christian hospitality differs from social entertaining. Entertaining focuses on the host: the home must be spotless, the food well prepared, the host must appear relaxed and good-natured. Hospitality, by contrast, focuses on the guests' needs, such as a place to stay, nourishing food, a listening ear, or just acceptance. Hospitality can happen in a messy home. It can happen around a dinner table where the main dish is canned soup. It can even happen while the host and the guest are doing chores together![2]

Hospitality can genuinely enrich the relationships in your life. It also allows you to be a leader and a server. During his public ministry, Jesus and his disciples depended entirely on the hospitality of others as they ministered from town to town.

Don't hesitate to offer hospitality just because you think you are too tired, too busy, or not wealthy enough to entertain. Have you ever made excuses for not being more hospitable? Have you heard your friends or family do this?

Let's take a closer look at some common excuses:

Excuse: I am too busy. I have so much to do.
Truth: We are all busy; remember, that to-do list is never going to end. But when your life is over,

it won't be the tasks that count. It will be the time spent with others and the impact you made on their lives that matter.

Excuse: My house isn't big enough.

Truth: You can always fit at least two other people in your space. Playing the comparison game is a recipe for disaster and another excuse.

Excuse: My house isn't clean enough or organized enough to have people over.

Truth: Generally, people don't care what your house looks like. They are just happy to get out of their own. If you are embarrassed about the lack of cleanliness or organization, do something about it. Planning a get-together is the perfect motivation to get your house in order.

Excuse: I can't afford to entertain.

Truth: You don't need much money. Coffee is cheap, and you can ask your guests to bring a snack to share to help offset the costs.

Excuse: I have social anxiety, or I am feeling too insecure lately.

Truth: If you are feeling anxious, be honest about it and stick with one-on-one meetups. We all have things that make us feel insecure, and that is OK. A good friend will lift and encourage you when you are feeling down. It is the best medicine for insecurity.

Excuse: I want to reach out to someone, but I am not sure how they will respond.

Truth: My friend, do not avoid sending an invitation because you are afraid to put yourself out there. I bet the other person is thinking the same thing. Be bold! If they do not want to put the effort in, you'll know this is not the type of friendship you need, and you can move on and invest in someone else.

Recently, I have heard much regarding church numbers and percentages. It seems our society is becoming less involved with our local churches. I have had this discussion with several people, and the consensus is that many of us need more from a church. I think what we are all in need of is more community. I am not talking about more social media; I am talking about *real*, sit-down, face-to-face discussions where we share ourselves with someone else. Times when we open up, laugh, cry, or seek advice. Where have these authentic conversations gone? To text messages, Facebook, and Voxer? You can't connect with a soul via an electronic device like you can in a cozy kitchen over a cup of coffee or on a soft sofa in front of a fireplace! Those are the places where deep bonds are formed.

Hospitality can turn your home and property into a ministry for people in the name of Jesus. Everything we have belongs to God and can be used for his glory. Your home is a gift. It is the one place in the entire universe in which you get to create an environment unique to you and the people you share it with. Everything from the decor to the entryway to the photographs on display speak about you and your family. Your home is a representation of you. So why not share that part of you with others?

Many people think ministry is something that happens away from home through church activities such as teaching Sunday school, setting up for a church event, or going on a mission trip. However, we don't even have to be associated with a religious organization to be in ministry. The word *ministry* simply means serving God and others. So if you are a believer, you have a ministry. How cool is that? You don't have to go to seminary or stand behind a pulpit; you just need to serve and love.

Take a Step

Some of my girlfriends and I were planning a get-together to make different kinds of protein balls. Kim said she would host because she has a gorgeous kitchen with a large island that we could all fit around. In the meantime, I wanted to create a blog post about making time for friendship. As I was doing the research, I found out there is actually a "holiday" called Galentine's Day. Say what? What is even more amazing is that I found out about this "holiday" the day before our protein-ball gathering (God is so good like that). When I arrived at Kim's house, I announced to everyone that we had a new holiday to celebrate! Here's a snippet from my post about making time for friends:

> Life is tough! You know that. And the only one that is going to get you and I mean REALLY get you is another woman. When that day comes, and you are crying on the floor because your marriage is on the rocks or you found out someone you love has cancer, you are going to need a friend. Maybe your teenager is going through something significant,

and you have no idea how to handle it. You are going to need a girlfriend to give you a pep talk. There will be days when you need her to remind you that you are strong, capable, and loved.

But having a relationship like that takes effort and time. And not just once or twice a year, I mean an intentional commitment to each other. Any good relationship takes this type of dedication and work. So how do we have relationships like this? We make time instead of making excuses.[3]

Not only are we called to be hospitable but we are also asked to do so with a smile on our face. Inviting people over and then begrudgingly cleaning up and making some snacks is not what God is talking about! I love how Donna Otto writes about this in her book *Finding Your Purpose as a Mom*:

> Your home is holy ground, remember. How you live in your most intimate spaces and with your closest relationships matters deeply for the kingdom of God. It's part of God's plan to change your life and then through you to change the world. . . . It's part of our sinful human nature to discount or underestimate or just not see what is simplest and most basic—closest to home, so to speak. It's human nature to value the exciting or dramatic or highly visible over the mundane and familiar, to want to "save the world" while neglecting what is right under our noses.[4]

We need to make hospitality a priority if we are serious about it. Are you ready to begin practicing hospitality more regularly? You can! Here are some tips on making hospitality easier.

1. Don't overthink it.

You don't have to be a Martha Stewart to entertain. If you have hot coffee and tea, water, and some snacks on hand, you are golden. If you don't, please do not apologize. When you begin by saying, "Don't mind the dishes," or "Sorry my house is such a mess!" you are not making your guests feel comfortable. They will sense your insecurity, and it will make them feel bad for intruding.

2. Be prepared.

You will be more comfortable when guests pop in or are invited over at the last minute if you are prepared. A few different types of drinks and bottled water, cheese and crackers, and fresh fruit and nuts are perfect items to have on hand.

3. Set a date.

I have often asked a client to set a date on the calendar to host a gathering at their house as a deadline for getting their home in order. If you want to get motivated to clean up your mess, invite people over!

4. Let go of perfectionism.

Most people will be so grateful for the invitation to come over and get away from the daily grind that they will never notice all the little things you see. They will just be ready to enjoy the time spent with you. Don't let the idea of a "perfect home" or "perfect meal" stop you from entertaining. If you open your doors, I guarantee God will open your heart.

5. Focus on making a memory.

Inviting guests over to do an activity together is a fun way to make new memories. You could host a cooking class, a Bible study, a book club, or a movie night. Choose any activity you would like to do, and then think of people you know who would be interested in doing it with you.

| Key Takeaway

Hospitality can genuinely enrich the relationships in your life and turn your home into a ministry. It also allows you to be a leader and serve. Don't hesitate to offer hospitality just because you feel too tired, too busy, or not wealthy enough to entertain.

TEN

Partner with God

Put GOD in charge of your work,
then what you've planned will take place.

Proverbs 16:3 Message

God gives us resources and opportunities to use for his work. When we manage these gifts wisely, he will provide us with even more resources and opportunities that can be used for an even greater harvest.

Friends, I have to let you in on a really, *really* important part of this journey for you: in order to live out your purpose, you need to learn how to make God your partner in this process. Actually, scratch that. You may very well get to live your purpose without God. For example, if your purpose is to rescue abused dogs and find them safe homes, you can absolutely do that on your own. But without God as your partner, you most likely won't reach the highest and purest potential within your purpose. Why? Because only God really knows what you are capable of doing. You may not even realize it yet, and that gets me super pumped up, because I cannot wait for you to find out how much potential lies within you. I have accomplished some things without God, but trust me, they were never as good or lasted as long as the things I have accomplished with him.

As an entrepreneur, I have always been good at finding and encouraging people to partner with me in various projects or business ventures. I have had several business partners, but last year a weird thing happened. First a business partner I had for eleven years came to me and wanted to sell the company that we built together. We had a good partnership and created a fantastic business, but suddenly her heart was no longer in it. Around the same time, I was splitting from the publisher I had been with for ten years and stepping down from a church committee I was on. My podcast partner also informed me that she could not keep up with the work, so I would have to keep going without her.

I am the type who always tries to understand "God's why," so I just kept praying for wisdom and understanding. At that time, one of my prayers in my journal went like this:

Dear Lord, why is all of this happening? Why is everything that I have known for the past decade or so changing? Why am I losing these partners? Is it because I am not trusting you to be my only partner? You have given me these gifts and visions; I need to trust you to help me use them for the world. Even people at church were influencing my opinions of what you are doing in my life. Lord, I only want to be directed by you! In Jesus's name, amen.

Not too long after this prayer, the answer came to me: God is my partner; with him *all* things are possible.

So I said yes to God. I kept that business and bought out my partner. I will tell you that the first event alone was scary—but a fantastic success. I was calmer and less anxious than I had been in years. Why? Because I was committed to putting my trust in my new Partner. I needed extra help, so my husband and children also stepped up, which made it feel more like a family-owned business. Another blessing!

I fought to get all of my rights back on my published books and won. God even placed the perfect attorney in my lap to help me do it, a Christian man. Coincidence? I think not! Little did I know at the time that this same man would become one of the first board members for Jennifer Ford Berry Ministries.

God also prompted me to launch the Created Order conference, and my daughter and her friends decided to start the Blurry conference for teens. One of the new Christian women I met introduced me to a company that could produce my podcast, which saved me loads of time.

Yes, God had an even bigger, more miraculous plan in store for me—and that was why all of this was happening.

Patient Partnership

There will be days when you get impatient on this journey, feel frustrated, or want to quit because you're tired and it's hard. Trust me; I have been there over and over again. But God's timing is perfect. (Personally, I have found it is easier to remember this after a dream comes true.)

When my husband, Josh, and I were trying to get pregnant with our second child, we thought it would be as simple as it was the first time.

Step 1: decide to get pregnant.

Step 2: try to get pregnant.

Step 3: find out you are pregnant.

Step 4: have a baby.

These steps worked perfectly with our daughter, so exactly two years later, when we wanted to have another child, I expected everything would occur the same way. Well, steps 1–3 happened like clockwork, but that step 4 did not. We were devastated when I went in for an appointment and the doctor told me I was going to have a miscarriage. We were told to go home and wait. I reminded myself that for centuries women had endured miscarriages naturally and that I could handle it, but it was horrible.

Then came another series of steps that ended in an ultrasound technician informing me that our third baby was no longer alive. Another devastating blow. So heartbreaking, in fact, that Josh did not want us to try again. He did not want me to have to go through the same experience, but I was not ready to give up on our dream. So, with a little trepidation and a *lot* of prayer, we tried again. This time I found out that my body was low on progesterone.

I didn't know if our hearts could withstand another loss, but then I met a pharmacist who told me he believed a specific medicine could help me stay pregnant. That man does not know this, but he gave me the best gift ever: hope. Not only did we end up having another baby but were blessed to have a son. Josh and I had hoped to have one boy and one girl since we dated in high school! The coolest part: Josh was the first to know it was a boy. In the middle of my C-section, he looked over the curtain (yes, he is in law enforcement, so he can handle stuff like this!) and saw that our baby was a boy. I will never forget the joy on Josh's face when he looked at me and said, "It's a boy!" I immediately started crying because I knew God had truly blessed us.

God knew his plan, and his timing was perfect. He knew what was behind that curtain. Does it break my heart that we lost two babies? Absolutely! But I know God meant for me to be Bryceton Richard Berry's mom, and if I had not gone through those heartbreaks, I would never know the joy of raising this cherished boy. As for our two other precious babies, I look forward to the day I can hold them in my arms in heaven.

Where to Begin

Here are some action steps to help you get serious about partnering with God to pursue your purpose.

1. Spend time with God daily.

To be led into a partnership with God, you have to spend time with him daily. Just as you would need to meet with other business partners, you have to make time in your schedule to meet with God. Ask God to speak to you, give you wisdom, and lead you to the right decisions. Trust me—this works. It is in these "meetings" with God that my jumbled brain of ideas always becomes bright with vision. It is also where I learn the most about God's ways of doing business, treating others, and accomplishing goals. He is my most exceptional mentor, and he wants to be yours too.

Even if you have not spent much time with God up until this point in your life, you can choose to start today. You may be asking, "How do I do this?" or "Where do I start?" and the answer is simple. Don't overthink it; just start with fifteen minutes per day reading the Bible (I highly recommend using a translation that is easy to understand), and perhaps listen to worship music while in your car. Remember, Jesus tells us to

> pay close attention to what you hear. The closer you listen, the more understanding you will be given—and you will receive even more. To those who listen to my teaching, more understanding will be given. But for those who are not listening, even what little understanding they have will be taken away from them. (Mark 4:24–25)

2. Enjoy the process of chasing your dreams.

How many times have you reached a goal, celebrated for a short time, and then moved on to chase a new goal? Over and over, right? That is life. When you were in college, you couldn't wait to get married. When you were married, you couldn't wait to buy your first house. When you bought your first house, you couldn't wait to have kids. When you started your career, there were tons of "next steps" you couldn't wait for.

The point is, life *is* the process. It is the everyday baby steps to get where you want to go. It is the daily moments when you don't give up. Don't miss out on those moments because you are so focused on the end result—because guess what, honey? After this goal there is always another. And another. The process you will go through prepares you for the promise God gave you.

3. Always be grateful.

When you find your purpose and live it wholeheartedly, boldly, and without apology, great things will begin to happen. At that point, be careful not to push God out of your life in order to give yourself all of the credit. Do not become too proud or too busy managing your success and wealth. Always remain focused on the One who provided you this opportunity and your abilities. It is God who gives us everything we have and who asks us to manage it for him.

4. Persevere.

As the writer of Hebrews tells us, "Patient endurance is what you need now, so that you will continue to do God's will. Then you will receive all that he has promised" (Heb. 10:36). Without such perseverance, you might not receive the promise God has given you. Anyone can give up. That's easy. But it takes endurance and perseverance to keep pushing yourself, day in and day out, when your progress isn't obvious or when your perspective gets blocked.

5. Be open and honest with God.

God already knows everything about you. You cannot hide from him. Let your guard down and be honest with him when you are frustrated, sad, or upset. He knows every thought before you think it, every decision before you make it. Talk about your choices with him and know that every right decision you make today can set you on a path to accomplish something significant.

6. Rest in God.

Finally, when you have done everything you know how to do, you have given it your all, and you are not sure what else you could do, rest in God. Remember, many dreams will not be accomplished alone. You are in need of help, and that help comes from the most loving and powerful Partner you could ever ask for.

You may be able to pull this "purpose" thing off by yourself, but can I give you a piece of advice? It will be a whole lot easier and a lot more fun—and a lot more effective—if you're partnered with God. What does that look like? Well, chances are the purpose you feel in your heart came straight from God and was placed there a long time ago. He gave it to you because he wants to make it come to fruition through you.

Repeat this prayer:

Lord, for that which I don't know, teach me. For that which I don't have, give me. For that which I am not, make me. All for the glory of heaven. Amen.

Key Takeaway

If you are excited to live a more purposeful and intentional life, the best thing you can do is spend time
meeting with God so that you will be able to discern
his will for your life.

Conclusion

The best reason for you to pursue your purpose more than your possessions is this: when you use your time and your gifts for God's ambitions, you will be filled with joy

As you embark on this new way of living, keep your eyes wide open to the ways in which God will show up and encourage you. Parting with physical clutter will open up new space for blessings. Your tastes will begin to change. You will notice God bringing new people into your life who are interested in growing, improving their lives, and making a difference. This will add more fuel to the fire of burning desire in your heart.

Having lived this experience myself, I have to tell you, friend, I am so excited for you! Up until this point, you may not have realized what you were missing—I know I didn't. But once you get a taste of a meaningful, purposeful life, nothing will ever satisfy you quite the same again.

Additional
Resources

If you need more advice about how to declutter, you can pick up one of my books in the Organize Now! series, available anywhere books are sold, including Amazon, and on my website, www.jenniferfordberry.com.

Organize Now! A Week-by-Week Guide to Simplify Your Space and Your Life (Great for helping you organize each area of your home.)

Organize Now! Think and Live Clutter-Free: A Week-by-Week Action Plan for a Happier, Healthier Life (Great for helping you clear away any clutter that is affecting your body, mind, and spirit.)

Organize Now! Your Money, Business & Career: A Week-by-Week Guide to Reach Your Goals (Great for organizing your business, finances, and goals.)

Additionally, *The 29 Minute Mom* podcast is my weekly show that offers motivation, inspiration, and organization for busy women.

Still not sure you are blessed enough to give? Check out this fantastic tool: http://www.globalrichlist.com/. You can enter your location and annual net income, and it will tell you how you rank against every other person in the world. For example, if you live in the United States and your annual net income is $50,000.00, you're in the top 0.31 percent of the richest people in the world by income.

Hospitality Checklist

God doesn't want you to feel overwhelmed and stressed out when you open your home to people you love, and neither do I. So in order to make this even easier for you, I've added my hospitality checklist. I hope this helps remove any stress you may have and also helps you to realize being hospitable is not hard. If you make your guests feel welcome and comfortable, then you are being a good host!

Tips

Keep your house in good shape. Guests will not feel welcome if you are completely stressed out and embarrassed about the condition of your home when they stop in. Make it a priority to do a quick pick-up before you go to bed or first thing in the morning to keep things tidy.

Always have items on hand in your pantry that you can pull out when you have company: napkins, tea, coffee, bottled water, crackers, dips, chips, premade cookie dough, iced tea mix, fresh fruit, and so on.

Premade party trays from the grocery store, deli, or bakery save a ton of food prep time.

Always get ready way before your guests are scheduled to arrive so you can be calm and welcoming.

Set the mood with great music and warm lighting, perhaps some candles.

Keep it simple. The important part of opening your home to others is to enjoy the time together and make them feel welcome.

If you are having guests stay overnight, make sure they have clean, soft bedding and extra pillows and blankets. It is a nice gesture to leave a small basket near the bed with items like a bottle of water, an eye mask, and body lotion. Also, don't forget to leave out clean towels and toiletries.

Make sure your pets are on their best behavior or put them in another room.

Try to cater to your company so that they feel welcomed. Try to have their favorite drink. If they are bringing children, make sure you have a basket of toys or something to entertain them.

How to Host a Party

Pick a date.

Decide on your guest list.

Write invitations and send them. (Make sure this is done two to six weeks ahead, depending on the type of party.)

Plan the food menu.

Choose the theme and decorations.

Decide what activities or games you want to include, if any.

Give your house a good cleaning the day before if the party is being held at your home, but do not worry about deep cleaning the spaces your guests will not be in. Focus on the main areas in which you will be entertaining.

Party Checklists

Setup

☐ Tablecloths
☐ Plates: large/small
☐ Bowls
☐ Cups: pop/coffee/beer
☐ Napkins/paper towels
☐ Plastic utensils
☐ Garbage bags
☐ Tape
☐ Scissors
☐ Coolers
☐ Can opener

☐ Extension cords
☐ Pot holders
☐ Dish soap
☐ Washcloths/dishtowels
☐ Coffee maker
☐ Bug spray/sunscreen (if the event is outside)
☐ Knives to cut rolls
☐ Bucket for water
☐ Plastic containers

Food

☐ Main dish
☐ Rolls
☐ Salads
☐ Sides
☐ Dessert

☐ Beverages
☐ Ice
☐ Condiments/dressings
☐ Salt/pepper

Notes

Introduction

1. Marsha Sinetar, *Do What You Love, the Money Will Follow: Discovering Your Right Livelihood* (New York: Dell Publishing, 1989).

Chapter 1 Possibilities

1. Kris Vallotton, *Poverty, Riches and Wealth: Moving from a Life of Lack into True Kingdom Abundance* (Bloomington, MN: Chosen, 2018), 48–49.

2. Thesaurus.com, s.v. "possibility," accessed November 16, 2021, https://www.thesaurus.com/browse/possibility.

3. Jennie Allen, *Made for This: 40 Days to Living Your Purpose* (Nashville: Thomas Nelson, 2019), 54.

4. Caroline Leaf, *Switch On Your Brain: The Key to Peak Happiness, Thinking, and Health* (Grand Rapids: Baker Books, 2013).

Chapter 2 Purpose

1. Sarah Jakes Roberts, *Don't Settle for Safe: Embracing the Uncomfortable to Become Unstoppable* (New York: Harper Collins, 2017), 129.

2. John Maxwell, "Quitting Is More about WHO You Are Than WHERE You Are," *John C. Maxwell* (blog), April 25, 2011, https://www.johnmaxwell.com/blog/quitting-is-more-about-who-you-are-than-where-you-are/.

3. *The 29 Minute Mom* podcast is available at https://jenniferfordberry.com/the29minutemom/.

Chapter 3 Possessions

1. Jen Hatmaker, *7: An Experimental Mutiny against Excess*, updated ed. (Austin: Hatmaker Partners LLC, 2017), 72.

2. Credit for this phrase goes to Gretchen Rubin, *Outer Order, Inner Calm: Declutter and Organize to Make More Room for Happiness* (New York: Harmony Books, 2019).

Chapter 4 Prepare

1. Merriam-Webster online, s.v. "prepare," accessed November 17, 2021, https://www.merriam-webster.com/dictionary/prepare.

2. John Maxwell, *Put Your Dream to the Test: 10 Questions to Help You See It and Seize It* (Nashville: Thomas Nelson, 2011).

Chapter 5 Plan Your Time

1. Elizabeth Gilbert, *Big Magic: Creative Living beyond Fear* (New York: Riverhead Books, 2015), 40–41.

Chapter 6 Part with Clutter

1. Jennifer Ford Berry, *Organize Now!: A Week-by-Week Guide to Simplify Your Space and Your Life* (Cincinnati: Betterway Books, 2010), 13.

2. Kristen McGrath, "The Big Picture: Decluttering Trends Report 2019," Offers.com, April 29, 2019, https://www.offers.com/blog/post/big-picture-decluttering-survey/.

Chapter 7 Practice Stewardship

1. Mike Richards, "STUFFOLOGY: The Theology of Stewardship," Crosspoint Church, November 28, 2016, https://www.cross-point.org/content.cfm?page_content=blogs_include.cfm&friendly_name=stewardship.

2. For more information about this course, visit "Financial Peace University," Dave Ramsey, https://www.daveramsey.com/store/product/financial-peace-university-class.

Chapter 8 Privileged Giving

1. "Global Water Crisis: Facts, FAQs, and How to Help," World Vision, accessed November 16, 2021, https://www.worldvision.org/clean-water-news-stories/global-water-crisis-facts.

Chapter 9 Provide Hospitality

1. Dictionary.com, s.v. "hospitality," accessed November 16, 2021, https://www.dictionary.com/browse/hospitality.

2. *NLT Life Application Study Bible*, 2nd ed. (Carol Stream, IL: Tyndale, 2011).

3. Jennifer Ford Berry, "Happy Galentine's Day," *Jennifer Ford Berry* (blog), accessed November 16, 2021, https://jenniferfordberry.com/galentines-day-are-you-too-busy-for-your-girlfriends/.

4. Donna Otto, *Finding Your Purpose as a Mom: How to Build Your Home on Holy Ground* (Eugene, OR: Harvest House, 2004), 226–27.

CONNECT WITH
JENNIFER

JENNIFERFORDBERRY.COM

 JenniferFordBerry   OrganizeNow

Created to give busy moms the inspiration, education, and motivation they need to get through another busy day.

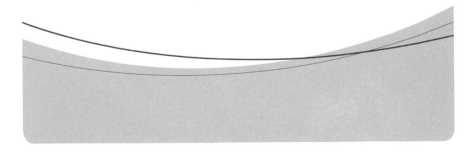